Leading
Continuous

CHANGE

Leading Continuous

CHANGE

Navigating Churn in the Real World

Bill Pasmore

Center for
Creative
Leadership®

BK

Berrett–Koehler Publishers, Inc.
a BK Business book

Berrett-Koehler Publishers, Inc.
1333 Broadway, Suite 1000, Oakland, CA 94612-1921
Tel: (510) 817-2277   Fax: (510) 817-2278   www.bkconnection.com

Ordering Information

Quantity sales. Special discounts are available on quantity purchases by corporations, associations, and others. For details, contact the "Special Sales Department" at the Berrett-Koehler address above.

Individual sales. Berrett-Koehler publications are available through most bookstores. They can also be ordered directly from Berrett-Koehler:

Tel: (800) 929-2929; Fax: (802) 864-7626; www.bkconnection.com.

Orders for college textbook/course adoption use. Please contact Berrett-Koehler:

Tel: (800) 929-2929; Fax: (802) 864-7626.

Orders by U.S. trade bookstores and wholesalers. Please contact Ingram Publisher Services, Tel: (800) 509-4887; Fax: (800) 838-1149; E-mail: customer.service@ingrampublisherservices.com; or visit www.ingram publisherservices.com/Ordering for details about electronic ordering.

Berrett-Koehler and the BK logo are registered trademarks of Berrett-Koehler Publishers, Inc.

Printed in the United States of America

Berrett-Koehler books are printed on long-lasting acid-free paper. When it is available, we choose paper that has been manufactured by environmentally responsible processes. These may include using trees grown in sustainable forests, incorporating recycled paper, minimizing chlorine in bleaching, or recycling the energy produced at the paper mill.

Library of Congress Cataloging-in-Publication Data
Pasmore, William A.
    Leading continuous change : navigating churn in the real world /
Bill Pasmore, Center for Creative Leadership.
        pages cm
    Includes bibliographical references and index.
    ISBN 978-1-62656-441-1
1. Organizational change—Management. 2. Organizational effectiveness.
I. Title.
    HD58.8.P367 2015
    658.4'06—dc23
                                                    2015013375

19 18 17 16   10 9 8 7 6 5 4 3 2

Cover design by Bradford Foltz. Interior design and composition by Gary Palmatier, Ideas to Images. Elizabeth von Radics, copyeditor; Mike Mollett, proofreader; Rachel Rice, indexer.

This book is dedicated to David Nadler.

You were a guiding force in the lives of so many.
We miss you, David.

Contents

Foreword

WHEN I WAS IN MY EARLY TWENTIES, the US Navy taught me how to fly airplanes. It took considerable study and work, as well as great coaches. Under their direction it was not long before my fellow rookie pilots and I were mastering takeoffs, landings, formation flying, and all the complex steps in between. Then they presented the next challenge: landing on aircraft carriers.

If you have never tried to do this, I'll tell you what an aircraft carrier looks like from 20,000 feet: pretty darn small. After a couple weeks of intense practice and feedback from our coaches, the moment of truth arrived: it was time to actually land on an aircraft carrier. That meant there was no room for error. Your only option was to bring the plane down exactly right.

Certainly, we trained hard for that moment. But in all honesty, no amount of practice on a runway can prepare you for landing on an aircraft carrier at sea. You have to account for shifting winds and the fact that the ship is rocking in the water, not to mention the tiny landing strip you're targeting. If you are planning to pull this off, you need to adapt and react—very, very quickly.

As I meet with the leaders of the many businesses, government agencies, non-governmental organizations (NGOs), and educational institutions that the Center for Creative Leadership

(CCL) is privileged to serve around the world, it strikes me that they are trying to do something quite similar to—and ultimately far more difficult than—landing on an aircraft carrier. They are trying to guide their organizations through an era of complexity and change that is unfolding at unprecedented speed, and finding the right place to land takes all the vision, skill, and courage they can muster. Like US Navy pilots soaring high above the ocean, they have no room for error. These executives need to get it exactly right. Their employees, clients, and communities are counting on that.

Yet all too often, disaster strikes.

Research shows that 50 to 70 percent of organizational change initiatives fail, wasting untold sums of talent, money, productivity, and opportunity. That is the story of the doomed DaimlerChrysler and AOL–Time Warner mergers and the disintegration of Polaroid. Even companies with very impressive track records, like Procter & Gamble and Walmart, have had to exit some countries where their usual recipe for success did not work.

Over the years in executive leadership roles with the US Navy, the State University of New York, and the Center for Creative Leadership, I have attempted to lead through the kinds of complexity that Bill Pasmore writes about in this book, and his guidance is right on the mark. Change initiatives fail, fundamentally, because leaders lack sufficient focus and a comprehensive plan. And that's usually because we are too consumed with the crisis of the day to take the necessary time to pause and reflect on the broader, deeper factors that will really determine longer-term results. As we say at CCL, leaders need to slow down to speed up.

And as with US Navy pilots, they need a great coach who can show them how to do that. Bill is that coach, and in this book he generously distills the remarkable wisdom he has gained over

40 years of researching, teaching, and consulting on change. For the better part of a decade, Bill has been a colleague of mine at CCL, where he has assisted numerous clients globally—many of them in the Fortune 500—with successfully navigating the complexities of change.

His opening advice for clients essentially boils down to this: check your ego at the door. The fact is that almost no one has done a great job of figuring out the intricacies of leading through continuous change, in large part because there's not a predictable formula for it. Every change initiative demands a customized approach that must first be created and then constantly adjusted as conditions evolve.

Bill cannot offer the Easy Button that the iconic Staples advertising campaign made popular, but in this book he does deliver an invaluable four-step framework for leading change. His emphasis on Discovering, Deciding, Doing, and Discerning offers a superb starting point for mapping out change initiatives in organizations of every size and type in any sector.

As a member of several corporate boards, I have learned the importance of stepping back and looking at the larger reality of what's happening in a business environment, which makes it possible to help leaders see things that they might ordinarily miss because they are too focused on narrow objectives. The process Bill describes equips every leader to take the stance of a board member, of someone who cares deeply about the success of the organization and is thus willing to challenge conventional thinking in search of bolder and smarter alternatives.

While leading change is the kind of topic that can easily elicit theoretical responses, Bill remains eminently practical, breaking the extremely challenging process of change into manageable increments that make the seemingly impossible finally approachable. And that is a welcome gift because the sooner business leaders understand and experiment with the principles of leading change, the sooner they can build better, more sustainable businesses for the benefit of everyone. Bill's trenchant insights, applied by the governments, NGOs, and educational institutions that are just as critical to the health of society, will help us build a better world, too.

> John R. Ryan
> President and CEO
> Center for Creative Leadership
> March 2015

Preface

I T HAS BECOME de rigueur to state that change is occurring in multiple
arenas, all at once, and faster than ever before in recorded history.
Leaders do not need to be told this. They are experiencing it
firsthand. What smart leaders want and need is a way to get ahead
of the curve. Instead of using every ounce of energy to just keep
up, smart leaders want to approach change in ways that continuously build positive energy, create greater change capacity, and
leave their organizations stronger. What's more, they want to
help their organizations make all the changes they should make
simultaneously, not just one or two or a few at a time. Change is
multifaceted and continuous. Smart leaders know they cannot
pretend otherwise.

Until now our approach to change has been built around
models that were developed with single changes in mind. We
assumed, because we had no alternative, that simply applying
these approaches to multiple changes occurring at the same time
would work. Then we discovered something we did not expect.
As we turned our attention to doing one change well, we took our
eye off another and another. People who assumed responsibility
for making individual changes were unable to get the resources
or support they needed to get the job done. In some cases, the
work on one change undid progress that had been made on

another. It became clear that we needed a better way to get on top of everything, but we weren't sure how. Some organizations appointed change czars to sort out the priorities and conflicts. This seemed to help a little, but then they discovered that a single czar could not stay on top of everything. If they appointed more czars, they just got in one another's way. What to do?

I have spent my entire career studying change, assisting with change, and leading change in organizations. For me and the organizations I work with, change equals improvement. We need to improve to remain competitive and to provide job security and returns to shareholders. We see that change is necessary, and most of us want desperately to succeed at it. Yet we know that change is not easy and improvement is not guaranteed.

It is painful to watch people start change efforts with great hope and later become overwhelmed by the difficulty or complexity of change. I have worked with chief executive officers (CEOs) and senior teams who are wholly dedicated to success, yet they still struggle. I've also worked with CEOs and teams who were not as committed. In these instances I sometimes become frustrated in my efforts to help them understand the difference between their stated intentions and actual behaviors.

What prompted me to write this book is that I wasn't as successful a change agent as I felt I needed to be. It's not that I lacked education, experience, or skill. I have been a scholar-practitioner in the field for almost 40 years, teaching at such institutions as Columbia, Stanford, INSEAD, and Case Western Reserve and working with organizations ranging from the Fortune Global 100 to small nonprofits. Rather, I found that the available approaches were inadequate to provide guidance to those who wanted to take on the world or to confront those who remained intentionally oblivious as the world around them changed.

As you will read here, change efforts fail between 50 and 75 percent of the time; our track record is simply unacceptable. Now, as we are confronted with even more and faster change, I have worried about our ability to keep up. We need to get better at change—much better—and we need to do so quickly. I have been inspired by some of my clients, who are taking steps to either get on top of change or stay ahead of it. You will read about some of them here.

I am in this work for the people who show up at the plant or office every day, trying to do a good job, and find that something about their organization is getting in the way of making things better. I'm in it for the leaders who want to serve those people by creating the most effective organizations in the world. I know that they can win—they being the leaders, the shareholders, the employees, and the customers—*only if everything works together.* We need the right talent, the right business models, the right systems and processes, the right leadership, and so forth. We also need agility because the world is changing at an accelerating rate in ways that are more and more important to us. What is "right" is constantly changing. We can't have these things unless we are capable of changing; and what's more, we can't reach our goal by changing just one thing at a time. We must learn to lead complex, continuous change.

If someone could give us a magic wand for successful change, we would take it. Faster change, less resistance, better execution—these are things we all desire. The material and approach presented here will not provide that magic wand, but you will learn something about what managing complex, continuous change requires and you'll pick up some new tools you can use. Mostly, this book does not feel like the final answer to me, but it does feel like progress. If we continue to experiment with the methods outlined here, we will learn and improve—and in this crazy world, perhaps that's as good as it gets.

By the way, if you are interested in taking a self-assessment on the mindsets introduced in this book as the foundation for leading continuous change, there is a link in Appendix B to the Leading Continuous Change Self-Assessment companion product. Progress begins with knowing where we are; this tool can help you understand the starting point for your journey.

1

Riding the Coaster

THINK BACK to your first roller-coaster ride. For some of you, it might have been on the Comet, one of the great wooden roller coasters of all time, nearly 100 years old and still in operation at the Great Escape in Queensbury, New York, after having been moved from its original location in Fort Erie, Ontario.

As you approached, the screams from those riding the coaster grew louder. What were you thinking? Was it going to be fun or terrifying? As you waited were you anxious to get to the front of the line, or were you looking around to find a way out? By the time you actually sat in the car and fastened your seat belt, were you excited or shaking?

Clank, clank, clank. As the cars climbed the first big hill, were you taking in the view with amazement or wondering how you got yourself into this mess? Did you have a premonition of doom (after all, you observed the first-aid office near the exit of the ride), or were you ready for whatever came? As you crested the first hill, did you relax going over the top or envision yourself falling off the moon and crash-landing into the park below, scattered into tiny pieces?

You were jolted from side to side. You may have wondered as you went up and down smaller hills and around curves if your seat belt was strong enough to hold you in. You had absolutely no clue where you were going or when the ride would end. Each corner brought a new surprise.

Obviously, you survived. Other than a few small bruises, you were fine physically, albeit perhaps a little nauseated (or *very* nauseated). Your legs wobbled for a little while once you got off, but it felt wonderful to be alive. You had done it.

Riding the coaster is an appropriate metaphor for living in a world of complex, continuous change. Sometimes we put ourselves in a position that leaves us exposed to unknown dangers, feeling vulnerable and out of control. We feel we don't have a choice. Standing pat is a recipe for failure. We are not sure how to get through what will happen next—and what a ride it is. We are surrounded by "churn"—everything is coming at us at once from every direction. We try to slow things down, sort it all out, and make good decisions, but we know that we're not on top of everything. More is happening than we could possibly have seen in advance. We want to believe we have things under control, but in a very real sense we are just along for the ride.

Neither avoiding change nor minimizing its importance is an optimal way to deal with complex, continuous change (triple-C). Neither cowards nor daredevils make great leaders of this kind of challenge. Others can tell you about their experiences in managing triple-C, but until you are the one in charge, you won't understand what it really feels like. You have to jump on board and live it. Like riding the Comet, only in hindsight will you be able to compare your imagination with reality.

If you have ridden the triple-C Comet and survived, you may believe that managing complex, continuous change is no big deal. You would be wrong, as the examples here of very intelligent leaders failing at complex, continuous change will show. You have developed an illusion of control that is simply not real. You believe that somehow, despite not knowing what will happen next, you will make the right decisions and manage your way through whatever comes your way. You believe that your choices will be the best available in the moment and that everything will work out eventually. This is a powerful delusion that is difficult to resist.

You recognize the upside of complex, continuous change. You know you can't learn much if you don't get on the coaster. You can't learn if you don't take some risks. Your organization stalls if you don't spend some time at the edge of your experience, trying something that is scary and new. You accept that you have to place some bets, aware that you may lose but not believing you really will. Instead of facing reality, you gamble that somewhere in the confusing morass of uninterpretable signals there is one that will eventually lead you forward and toward success in a big way. You tell yourself that leadership is not for the weak and that you are strong. Despite being rocked violently from side to side, you are in command. You can handle it. You will survive. But in actuality, not everyone does survive in the real world of triple-C. The truth: business is not just a ride after all.

If a crash actually occurs, it is a shock and you meet it with either disbelief or resignation. A business plan that has worked for decades suddenly breaks down, or your best-selling product is eclipsed by someone else's innovation. Or someone you trust does something you never imagined him capable of doing. The real world is not an amusement park. It can be a surprisingly harsh and unforgiving place. You may walk away, but not without a tarnished reputation and not without others suffering harm.

If, on the other hand, your early experiences with complex, continuous change were negative, you may have developed an aversion to change. You may now put all of your energy into protecting your organization from the world. While you tell yourself that you are being prudent, you are actually putting yourself and others at risk. Experts tell us that more organizational failures occur from avoiding change than from attempts to change successfully.[1]

Blockbuster Video stores and Borders bookstores stayed committed to their bricks-and-mortar strategies when the world was shifting to digital entertainment. Kodak and Polaroid remained in silver-halide photography, in part due to the investments they had made in their chemical film–producing operations. American Motors and Chrysler were unable to withstand the onslaught of lower-priced and then higher-quality foreign competition. Lucent Technologies was too slow to move from mechanical network telephone switching to cheaper digital switches; and both Wang and Digital Equipment gave up leadership positions in their industries to competitors that included Apple, Hewlett-Packard (HP), Dell, and IBM. Speaking of IBM, everyone knows that the reason the brand survives today is that its then-CEO, Lou Gerstner, drove a change in the company's focus from hardware to services. HP's attempt to follow suit was slower and not as successful. There are many more examples, but the point is that none of these companies wanted to die; in fact, they wanted to live and they thought that the best way to do so was to stay focused on what had worked for them in the past rather than taking a bold step into the unknown. So long as they still had *some* customers, it must have seemed like a return to profitability was just around the corner. Perhaps a new advertising campaign or a redesigned product would save them.

They hoped for the best, but the truth could not be denied. They played it safe, which turned out not to be a safe thing to do at all.

Somewhere between the extremes of using all of your power and influence to protect the status quo by trying to stop change from happening and completely abandoning reason to simply "let whatever happens happen" lies the right way to lead an organization through complex, continuous change. There are many phrases to describe those who try to avoid or stifle needed change: *sticking your head in the sand, being risk-averse, putting your finger in the dike, hanging on to the past, being out of touch with reality, wishing for the good old days, being too committed to your course of action, ignoring the cues, locked-in, looking in the rearview mirror, sliding into a death spiral.* There are also names for those who are too quick to jump at each opportunity change presents: *foolhardy, fast and loose, overly aggressive, prone to snap judgments, thrill seeking, undisciplined.* What do we call those who have discovered how to manage effectively the inherent tradeoffs in complex, continuous change? *Pioneers, change leaders, visionaries, balanced, intuitive, successful.* This is the group in which you want to be.

If you are one of these leaders, you seek ways to reduce the risks that accompany complex, continuous change. You have gained awareness of your capacity to manage this kind of change and the capacity of others around you. You build in more safeguards by following sound change practices and increasing the processing ability of your organization to make good decisions in the moment and learn from them. You ride with your eyes open, steering the coaster instead of just going along for the ride.

If you work hard and long at learning how to lead complex, continuous change, you improve. You ascend to a position of dominance in your industry that forces others to follow your lead, eventually causing their downfall if they choose not to learn from your example. You get to control your fate.

Whether you are leading complex, continuous change or advising those who do, you must understand what is required of you to succeed. You need to be willing to revise your way of thinking about change. You also need to understand how to tell when you have exceeded your capacity to change and recognize that continuing at your current course and speed will not lead to the outcomes you desire. You will need to learn greater discipline and focus, how to think in terms of scarcity rather than abundance, and how to slow down to get faster at change. Only leaders can make the critical decisions that determine how the ride will end.

We're Playing a New Game

The field of organizational development was conceived by behavioral scientists as a way of helping organizations introduce planned change. Changes to work practices, strategy, organizational design, mergers and acquisitions, and so forth were too often resisted by those whose help was required for them to succeed. Kurt Lewin, the most widely recognized progenitor of the field, in the 1940s and '50s laid out the basics of what became the backbone for change work in organizations. His model was simple and intuitive. It called for leaders to (1) "unfreeze" the organization by clarifying the need for change; (2) introduce change using highly participative methods that allowed others to see for themselves the logic and necessity of change and even to contribute to the design of the change itself; and (3) "refreeze" the organization by institutionalizing new ways of working through the adoption of new methods, policies, and procedures that would not allow it to relapse into comfortable but ineffective ways of operating.

Later others added to Lewin's three steps. It was recognized, for example, that before the leader could help others change, the leader himself had to be committed to the change. If a leader refused to acknowledge the clear need for change, engaging him in learning about the threats or sharing with him the results of careful diagnoses could increase his readiness to act.

If a leader had difficulty getting her staff on board with the change, techniques were developed to understand people's concerns and address them. Using surveys to gather opinions and then summarizing the data so that it could be discussed by leaders and employees in a search for solutions became an extremely popular approach. In other cases, when the implementation of good ideas failed to happen, reward systems were realigned to provide incentives for desired new behaviors. Over the years literally hundreds of techniques and approaches for managing change were invented, ranging from individual coaching to large-scale interventions involving thousands of people simultaneously. Despite the proliferation of approaches to managing change, the planned change success rate has remained stuck at around 30 to 40 percent.

John Kotter's eight-step model, introduced in 1996, became the most widely cited roadmap for changing organizations:[2]

1. Increase urgency.

2. Build the guiding coalition.

3. Get the vision right.

4. Communicate for buy-in.

5. Empower action.

6. Create short-term wins.

7. Don't let up.

8. Make change stick.

Kotter's approach followed Lewin's basic framework, which is premised on a *linear* notion of how *single* changes occur.[3]

But at about the same time that Kotter's model was published, others were questioning whether Lewin's linear, single-focused thinking could still be applied successfully to the world we live in today. Peter Vaill was among the first and most vocal to articulate this alternative point of view. His 1989 book, *Managing as a Performing Art: New Ideas for a World of Chaotic Change,* struck a chord with beleaguered managers who could not keep up with the changes occurring around them.[4] Just as one change was introduced, another was needed, and often that change required undoing something the previous change had accomplished. Under these circumstances orderly steps and one-at-a-time sequential changes went out the window. One explanation for why all the tools and techniques that were devised to help with change were not actually helping is that there was simply too much change going on. Tools designed to manage one change at a time could not keep up with the constant interruptions that came from the need to change course continuously.

What Vaill called "permanent whitewater" we refer to here as *complex, continuous change,* that is, *a series of overlapping, never-ending, planned and unplanned changes that are interdependent, difficult to execute, and either cannot or should not be ignored.* Organizations facing triple-C can reach the point of *change saturation* in which the many important changes that must be undertaken can no longer be addressed through parallel, linear, sequential change efforts. Changes start falling off the plate because there are not enough resources to address them, and organizational performance suffers as more effort is put into transformation and less is left over to support ongoing operations. What is a leader living in a world of complex, continuous change to do?

Recently, at a conference that addressed the topic of change, Kotter made the statement that a new approach to change was needed to keep up with the pace and complexity of change that we are experiencing. He said that while his model still makes sense when we focus on a single-change effort, as the pace and complexity of change exceeds our capacity to respond effectively, a new approach to change must be invented. We are playing a new game.

One idea that has been suggested is to take Lewin's ideas around involvement a step further and get everyone involved in making change happen rather than leading change from the top. The theory is that by getting more people involved, there would be greater shared understanding of what should happen, fewer up and down the hierarchy meetings needed to clarify things, and more hands on deck who are committed to assist. Further, there would be greater buy-in and fewer conflicts due to one part of the organization's fighting with another about the direction of change. Marvin Weisbord, in his 1987 book *Productive Workplaces*, laid out the tenets for an approach to change that "got the whole system in the room."[5] Building on the earlier work of Fred Emery and Eric Trist on "search conferences," the idea was to eliminate the "strategizing at the top and execution at the bottom" that often leads to change failures.[6] While these ways of managing complex, continuous change were a step forward, they were not entirely successful. It turns out that it's easier to get the whole system *into* a room than to get the whole system to do something after people *leave* the room.

These whole-system or "large-group" interventions, including popular variations like the appreciative inquiry summits and the world café, are sometimes run as onetime, single-focus events.[7] They can also be repeated over time and in different parts of an organization or system. Using these methods, change leaders have discovered that they can indeed get more people in the room to increase understanding of the whole system before they target specific changes to be made. They also discovered, however, that follow-through from whole-system events is a challenge and that only rarely do these discrete events build upon one another to produce continuous adaptation. Even with many people involved, our single, linear interventions are simply not agile enough to deal with the many complex changes we are facing. Nor can we do them frequently enough to keep up with the pace of change around us.

Another suggestion that has been offered is to devote attention to one key change effort at a time. There *are* success stories of narrowly focused sustained linear change programs, and we should not overlook them because they inform us of conditions that are required to achieve footholds as we climb toward higher levels of organizational performance. The Work-Out program developed by General Electric (GE) that brought people from a unit together to identify and eliminate unnecessary tasks, the high-performance manufacturing systems of Procter & Gamble (P&G) that relied on people's becoming more skilled and making more operational decisions for themselves, and Toyota's lean manufacturing system that eliminated inventory and controlled for quality—all are examples of effective focused-change efforts that stuck for more than a decade.[8]

Clear sustained leadership, commitment to a common underlying approach, and many internal change agents trained in the same methodology are hallmarks of these efforts. Each of these focused programs addressed an important challenge but certainly not all the challenges that these organizations were facing. It could even be argued that placing too much effort into a single-change program detracted from paying attention to other important changes that should have been taking place. GE, P&G, and Toyota knew very well that to become agile they needed more than a single signature program. The successful completion of any single program does not mean that the need for change is sated. Instead we simply must move past a series of one-shot interventions and embrace the need for continuous change without overwhelming ourselves and losing control.

The "over time" part of change is especially challenging. In a world of complex, continuous change, making changes stick is difficult and perhaps not even the right thing to do. Factors that threaten the sustainability of change efforts include leadership turnover, strategic combinations (takeovers, mergers, acquisitions), competitive challenges, burnout, resistance, and failure to demonstrate compelling outcomes. Making and sustaining change in the face of these forces is not easy. No wonder our success rate for single planned-change efforts remains around 30 percent.

If we try to undertake multiple change efforts simultaneously using an approach designed for single changes, doing everything that is required and keeping our efforts coordinated becomes more challenging. We jump from one change effort to another before we complete the first. We change directions, waste time and resources, and fall further behind. We are playing a new game, and we need new ways to play it.

More Important Than Ever, but Still Struggling to Succeed

Three things make the changes organizations face today different from those of even two decades ago. First, the speed with which change is occurring is increasing, largely due to the second factor, which is the influence of technology on nearly every aspect of doing business. The third factor is globalization, which has arrived and is making standing pat an almost certain recipe for obsolescence. The most dramatic changes show up in two key areas: mergers and business failure rates. The turnover of companies in the Fortune 500 has been thoroughly documented.[9] Even large, powerful institutions are dropping from the scene at alarming rates. Many of them succumb to acquisitions, which themselves are documented by independent studies performed by McKinsey and KPMG to fail two-thirds of the time.[10] Specifically, these reports cited "soft issues," such as selecting the right leadership team for the combined entity, resolving cultural issues, and communicating effectively, as key to success but frequently overlooked.

There is a natural evolution of business that makes some competitors less viable, leading to their replacement by younger, stronger firms. Should American Motors have been bailed out by the US government as General Motors (GM) was decades later? What about bailouts for TWA and Braniff airlines? Many would say no; these companies were past their prime and should have been allowed to perish, as they would have needed continuous propping up in the face of growing competition from

Toyota, British Airways, and others. Yet the view from inside was undoubtedly different. While paddling against the current, did these companies have fatal flaws, or were they simply incapable of making the changes required to evolve? Certainly, when investors lose faith, little can be done. But what separates a Packard from a GM, or a Swissair from a Virgin Atlantic? At some point in their evolution, they had roughly equal prospects. Without a crystal ball, you would not have known which stock to buy for your retirement portfolio. And yet some of these classic competitors survived while others did not. One possible explanation is that some of these companies were better than others at dealing with change.

The passage of time has not made things simpler. If anything, the competitive environment has become even more challenging—faster, more technology driven, and increasingly global. As China, India, and Brazil become increasingly business-savvy, it will take more innovation and change for others to adopt effective counterstrategies. After facing decades of low labor costs, rapid duplication of technological advances, and government support for business expansion from these competitors, firms in the United States and Europe have been challenged to improve their operations in every respect. If there ever was enough time to sit back and figure things out from within the walls of an impenetrable castle, there certainly is not now.

So, while the speed and scope of global, technology-fueled change has increased, our ability to respond has not. More-complex and demanding changes, like merger integration, installing enterprise resource planning (ERP) systems, and venturing into global expansion, have high failure rates, even among some of our best companies. As change has become more critical and complex, many companies are still struggling to find the right approaches to ensure positive outcomes. This should be a wake-up call to all of us. We need to get better at leading complex, continuous change, and we need to do so as quickly as we can.

A Few Examples of Gigantic Change Failures

Organizations fail when they run out of money and other resources. But going bust is the end of the story, not the beginning. There are many reasons why organizations run out of funds, but the two primary culprits are failure to recognize the need for change and failing at change. Failing to recognize the need for change can arise from complacency, irrational exuberance, or events that are beyond control (natural disasters, for example). These failures are important to understand but have already been detailed in such books as Clayton Christensen's *The Innovator's Dilemma* and George Day and Paul Schoemaker's *Peripheral Vision: Detecting the Weak Signals That Will Make or Break Your Company*.[11] Here we are more concerned with the second cause of failure, which is failing *at* change.

In the examples that follow, leaders passed the first test; they became aware of the need for change and were attempting to drive forward strategies that would respond to the challenges and opportunities before them. They failed the second test, however, which was to complete the complex, interrelated, simultaneous changes that were required to achieve success. These well-documented illustrations are only the tip of the iceberg; they reflect a much larger population of change failures around the globe that together are wasting billions of dollars and billions of hours. By studying these efforts, we can learn lessons that will aid us in changing more effectively.

Sensational Mergers That Failed Sensationally: DaimlerChrysler and AOL–Time Warner

Why have the DaimlerChrysler and AOL–Time Warner mergers become the benchmark against which bad strategic combinations are measured? They were large and visible, to be sure. They were household names, and each combination held promise for producing dramatic shifts in how the combined organizations could attack the market. Still, these are not unique promises. What makes them stand out, in my view, is that we *expected* them to be much better managed and much more successful than they were. Each merger received high praise from business pundits and Wall Street analysts before it happened. All four organizations involved were led by savvy businesspeople. The mergers *should* have worked, but didn't.

In the various autopsies that were conducted, the explanation offered most frequently was simple: their cultures didn't fit together. Although true, part of the logic for the combinations in the first place was that their cultures were unique and supposedly complementary. Leaders on both sides thought that they would be able to leverage their cultures to help the other do more than it could have done alone. But in the end, they couldn't.

In so many failed mergers, the blame is placed on poor social integration rather than poor strategy. A report issued by McKinsey more than a decade ago said as much.[12] It is not difficult getting the expense duplication or "synergies" out of the combined organization. That is as simple as laying off people and closing redundant offices. No, it turns out the harder part is getting key people to stay and work together productively and aligning systems and processes to serve customers.

An overly simplistic explanation of why sensational mergers fail sensationally is that the people leading the effort look at the merger as *an event rather than a process.* If you consider a merger an event, the work is done when the papers are signed. Cleaning up afterward is considered, in this view, a simple matter of appointing some people to be in charge, letting others go, and deciding whose information technology (IT) systems will be used for accounting and e-mail.

If instead you understand that consolidation is not an event but rather a process, you know that signing the papers is when the real work begins. In actuality, mergers involve complex, continuous change over time. Think about some of the things that need to happen for the merger to deliver its promised returns: cost savings have to be generated; leaders need to be appointed and gain the trust and confidence of those who must follow them; technical processes and IT systems must be melded together seamlessly; customers and other stakeholders need to receive communications to help them understand how to interact with the new combined organization; duplicate sales forces have to be consolidated without disrupting customer relationships; a single culture must be created that welcomes each person's contributions regardless of previous loyalties; and boards of directors may need to be consolidated.

This list is only the beginning. As changes work their way into the organization, efforts at every level and eventually by every team must be made to understand the significance of the change and its implications. Because all of this must happen during the same period of time, the change is both complex and continuous.

The DaimlerChrysler and AOL–Time Warner examples are not intended to indicate that mergers are a bad idea. Rather, in these cases, the mergers were strategically challenging and therefore complex. Bringing different cultures and different business models together under one roof is not in itself wrongheaded. Yet leaders must recognize the risk when two entities that are not at all alike are expected to find ways to work together. The DaimlerChrysler and AOL–Time Warner deals were not doomed from the start, as those with the benefit of perfect hindsight might wish to believe. Instead it was an underestimation of the challenge involved and a consequent mishandling of the integration process that led to the sad endings that ultimately occurred.

Staying on top of everything that must change, focusing on the correct priorities, and not allowing an integration effort to completely disrupt ongoing operations is a huge challenge. The difficulty is exacerbated by people from each company not liking one another, as in cases where "the cultures don't fit together" or when people come from different professional backgrounds (such as print versus digital). What seems straightforward from a distance appears a daunting challenge close-up.

Mergers and acquisitions are not bad ideas. Many of them have been done successfully by companies like Cisco and more recently Yahoo!, which seem to have mastered the social integration process. Yet overall nearly two-thirds of business combinations still fail, mostly because we are not fully prepared to handle the complex, continuous change that mergers and acquisitions involve.[13]

Can There Be Too Much Innovation? The Case of Polaroid

It can safely be said that at one time Polaroid was the most creative company in the world.[14] Its dazzling innovations in polarization and instant photography, led by founder Edwin Land, caught the attention of consumers and investors alike. The story of the company's growth is truly a tribute to Land's genius. Before he was finished, Land held more patents than anyone in history except Thomas Edison, and it could be argued that many of his patents were much more complex. Yet Land's prowess as an inventor led to the company's eventual demise.

Innovation is always a hit-or-miss proposition, and yet many companies rely on successful innovations for their continued survival. Those who believe that the process of innovation can be designed and managed to produce outputs like a predictable production line have never been close to the action. Even elaborate stage-gate models that many organizations use to make decisions about where to invest their innovation dollars do not guarantee success. Stage-gate models help us choose among innovations, but the creation of the innovations themselves is still more art than science. One never knows when the next breakthrough will come.

Not knowing when or whether you will succeed at a task that is critical to survival introduces complexity. Innovation leaders face a continuous stream of decisions that they must make based on partial information. Bets are placed before concepts are fully tested. Investments are made in research, development, manufacturing, and distribution only to later discover that things don't go as planned and that other, potentially more attractive alternatives have emerged. Leading an organization that runs on innovation requires that you understand something about dealing with complex, continuous change.

At Polaroid, Land had done this for years. From one unimaginable success to the next, he seemed to have the golden touch. His reputation for accomplishing what others thought impossible grew, as did sales. Few on the board were prepared to challenge his decisions given his role as founder and inventor of all that Polaroid had become.

Unfortunately, with success, Land's ego also grew. He became convinced that only he could see the future and that others who warned him against taking certain actions were simply not his equals. Such was the case when Land decided to bet everything on inventing a chemically based process for taking instant movies, even as videotape was emerging as a product in the commercial realm. Despite strong warnings from his closest advisers, Land underestimated how quickly videotape would evolve from an expensive product that only businesses could afford to a ubiquitous and moderately priced consumer good. His own product, although capable of allowing consumers to take instant movies, was inferior and inflexible in comparison to digital photography's recording and playback capabilities. Land won his personal battle to bring the product to market, but he lost the war. The losses associated with Land's big bet were the beginning of the end for Polaroid. Land was ousted, and those who followed were overtaken by the shift from chemical to digital photography.

Although this story is not repeated often, lesser versions of failing to manage complex change during innovation occur frequently. Some leaders get locked into ideas, chase imaginary deadlines, disregard negative signals, and ignore the outside world as they try to recover sunk costs. They trust their experience to guide them rather than listen to what others are trying to tell them.

When innovating, we shouldn't shut out information about the world. Instead we need to be open to learning and prepared to change directions as the situation dictates. Pharmaceutical companies that have deep expertise in the formulation of chemically based drugs know that they must consider shifting into biologics and gene therapies. Educators recognize the need to adopt new curricula. Almost every business has considered how to take advantage of the opportunities the Internet provides to create new business models. Still many are failing to make the changes they know are necessary. Concluding that you are headed in the wrong direction and doing something about it are different things. Your speed of response is essential, as is understanding how to manage complex, continuous change.

Going Global: Procter & Gamble Enters Brazil, and Walmart Enters Germany

The market for business and consumer goods has gone global. It's not surprising that large companies want to expand their markets into new territories to find sources of growth that compensate for slower growth in markets where saturation and fierce competition have eroded profit margins. The challenges associated with "going global" are often underestimated. As in the cases of mergers and innovation, some leaders who should know better believe that going global is as simple as replicating what has worked elsewhere. Procter & Gamble and Walmart—huge firms with long histories of success—learned that following a formula when entering a new market is not always a recipe for winning. Each had to pull out of countries it tried to enter in the face of stiff competition, government regulation, and consumer disinterest. Disney nearly failed in France but is slowly turning around its European operation after learning a great deal about how different cultures prefer to be fed and entertained. Disney learned and then went on to do much better in its expansion into Japan.

Going global automatically creates complexity that must be managed. Adapting products to fit the local market is only the first step. Working within the legal structures of other countries requires adaptation; distribution channels must be established;

talent must be hired and trained; determining where the power to make operational decisions rests is a frequent source of conflict between headquarters and regional leaders; translating internal and external documents is harder than one might imagine; learning from local experiences and responding to the moves of local competitors requires continuous adjustment; political conflicts disrupt plans; and so on.

We are going global and will continue to do so, but we must be smarter about what that entails and better about managing the complex, continuous change that is necessary.

Improving Operations: Hershey's ERP and Royal Bank of Canada's Outsourcing

In 1996 Hershey's began installing a new enterprise resource planning system to reduce costs, increase efficiency, and modernize its IT infrastructure. Like many others, Hershey's discovered that switching to a new ERP system required more than hiring external consultants and waiting for them to "flip the switch." The reason that the Hershey's case stands out is that the failure to implement the new system on time caused major problems with delivering products to customers, resulting in a 12 percent drop in quarterly revenues compared with the previous year.

Almost every enterprise that has undergone a major reengineering effort, including the installation of a new ERP system, can tell stories about delays, cost overruns, and performance promises that were not kept. Software vendors and consultants will explain that the delays were due not to issues on their side but rather to the failure of the enterprise to provide the support or clear direction needed for work to be done on time. They aren't wrong. Few organizations are fully prepared for the magnitude of the changes involved in such efforts. Not long after commencement, it becomes clear that the systems being redesigned and automated require process changes, not simply plugging data into computers. These process changes require changes in job responsibilities, job descriptions, capabilities, rewards, and even in some cases organizational design. Once it is in place, maintaining and updating the system requires constant attention. There are costs associated with all of this as well as disruptions to operations. A single change triggers the need for multiple changes in the systems that it touches. What appears straightforward is much more complex than imagined.

Because the magnitude and complexity of the change is underestimated, resources are not budgeted appropriately. Cost overruns are the result. In addition, because some leaders believe they can outsource to vendors the design and installation of new systems, they fail to plan for the attention that will be required of their own people. They add the extra work required on top of other responsibilities, only to find that people become overloaded and something else suffers. Change is not free, even when outsourced.

At Royal Bank of Canada (RBC), a simple change became a complex one as a decision was made to outsource IT work to India, resulting in the reduction of about 40 positions in Canada. That in itself is certainly not news; outsourcing has become common practice. What was different in this case was how the change was handled. The employees who were being let go were asked to train their Indian replacements, who came to Canada on temporary work permits that may or may not have been acquired properly (this is still being contested). The long-term employees' outrage caught the attention of the media, which raised questions about the bank's commitment to providing work for Canadians and its sensitivity to the feelings of its employees. It seemed a clear case of greed: a huge, successful, profitable institution saving a few dollars at the expense of the little guy. RBC tried to improve its image by investing in charitable activities, and perhaps not surprisingly the CEO resigned.

The lesson from Hershey's and RBC is that even when business leaders think changes will be simple and straightforward, they can become much more complex than imagined. We should never think that one change will not affect anything other than what it is designed to do. Organizations exist in an ecosystem of ongoing relationships with their employees, customers, partners, investors, and communities. It is impossible to isolate changes into neat compartments that do not touch other elements of this ecosystem.

Nor should we ever presume that because a change went well in another organization it will go smoothly in ours. Seemingly simple changes can easily get out of hand, demanding much more time, money, and attention than we predict. When this happens with multiple changes that are occurring at the same time, the result is a systemwide change breakdown, sometimes with catastrophic results.

Adopting New Strategies: Lehman Brothers and Bank of America/Merrill Lynch

It is fashionable and necessary to adopt new business strategies and business models as markets evolve. Given the increased speed with which the world changes and the heightened competition to exploit new ideas that generate growth, it is not surprising that organizations sometimes adopt strategies that are not fully pressure tested. It's move or die; but a wrong move can be disastrous, as Lehman Brothers found out.

In the years leading up to its 2008 bankruptcy, Lehman leveraged heavily to buy into real estate, leaving it vulnerable to a turndown in the housing market. This was compounded by Lehman's taking a strong position in the subprime mortgage market, the sector most likely to fail under such circumstances. On losses of $2.8 billion in the second quarter of 2008, the value of Lehman stock decreased by 73 percent. Lehman tried to sell its assets to several other banks but ultimately could not. Bankruptcy was the inevitable result. The government chose not to step in, and Lehman was allowed to disappear, in turn affecting its customers, including nearly a hundred hedge funds that used Lehman as their prime broker. The global fallout was massive, helping trigger a deep worldwide recession that lasted several years.

Usually, when strategies fail, organizations simply write off the losses and move on. In this case the losses were too big; Lehman literally bet the bank on the subprime mortgage strategy. Overconfidence? Misinformation? Poor decision making? A profound disregard for goodwill? There are several competing explanations for what happened at Lehman. What is undeniable is that no strategy is *guaranteed* to work in a world that is as interconnected and volatile as the one we live in today. The idea that a strategy *will* work can become so compelling that, like the other missteps we've discussed, we can oversimplify the challenges associated with execution. We want the strategy to work, but we don't understand fully what it will take to make it work or what factors are legitimate threats to its success. As a result, we don't pay attention to warning signs, listen to the voices or critics, or prepare satisfactory escape options.

Leading strategists like Rita McGrath from Columbia Business School rarely talk about "formulating a strategy" anymore.[15]

They know that the idea that a strategy can be formulated and executed without needing to adapt it over time is outdated. In a world of complex, continuous change, experts like McGrath, Donald Sull, Shona Brown, and Kathleen Eisenhardt now emphasize that capturing a strategy on paper is only the starting point of a complex change effort that will continue for as long as the strategy is pursued.[16] No matter who formulates the strategy or how much we pay for it, no one can predict the future. As soon as we start executing, the world will change. That's why long, expensive strategy building can become a trap. We feel that we have invested so much time, money, and effort into developing the strategy that we must continue to pursue it, even when there is clear evidence that it no longer makes sense. Instead we should, as Steven Krupp and Paul Schoemaker tell us, invest in strategy as an ongoing learning process.[17]

Why Change So Often Fails

There are many reasons why change efforts fail. In an earlier article, I reviewed more than 50 years of research in the field of organizational development and noted the most frequent challenges we encounter when undertaking change.[18] These fell into four broad phases of change efforts:

- ▶ Understanding the need for change
- ▶ Framing the change
- ▶ Undertaking the change
- ▶ Sustaining the change

In the first phase, we run into challenges of identifying the need for change and its importance. We make too much or too little of the need for change, and we try solutions that are familiar but not appropriate under the evolving circumstances. Our commitments to change lack true conviction, leading to abandonment later on.

In framing the change, we set the scope of the change too broadly or too narrowly. We fail to align important stakeholders or get early input from key people in the organization about factors that could affect success. We allow consultants to lead us down the wrong path by advocating approaches that they are pushing rather than what we really need. And we don't assess readiness before we advance.

Examples? Both G. Richard Thoman at Xerox and Carly Fiorina at HP ran into staunch resistance when as outsider CEOs they declared that the cultures of their companies were barriers to progress. Both made their people and their boards uncomfortable, leading eventually to their replacement by CEOs who embraced what their companies' cultures had to offer. Ann Mulchahy, who took over Xerox from Thoman, was a longtime insider who understood how to bring out the best in Xerox's people. She had a stellar run as CEO before passing the reins to another longtime insider, Ursula Burns.

Once we undertake the change, we run into a host of issues. As leaders we may find that we are not prepared for our roles and have underestimated the personal challenge. Or we discover that the change will be more difficult than imagined because we uncover issues that we should have known about before we began. It could be that as things progress, we realize we are going down the wrong path but have difficulty adjusting due to the investment in our original plans.

My review of change obstacles was based on research and case studies involving, for the most part, single changes. As we step back from the details of single-change efforts and look instead at the reality of complex, continuous change, we multiply the degree of difficulty exponentially. Each of the individual efforts that make up complex, continuous change faces its own challenges, but together they create interference for one another. People quickly become overloaded, have difficulty sorting out what is really important, and complete for the resources required for implementation. The need to work through the overlaps among projects results in more "change overhead"—meetings that eat up time but do not advance progress.

So You Think You're Better Than Everyone Else at This?

While there is evidence to suggest that between half and two-thirds of change efforts fail, we know that we must continue to introduce change or face the consequences of falling behind.[19] No one sets out to fail at change. Yet it is too easy to believe that we will succeed where others have failed. We shouldn't guess at whether our organizations are prepared to succeed at managing complex, continuous change. We should collect data to assess readiness and capability rather than rely strictly on a gut feeling.

It is true that many changes proceed without a hitch. They are usually the easier ones that few people oppose. The more difficult changes are ones that that disturb what people do, where they do it, who they do it with, or the rewards they receive.

The reasons why these more difficult efforts fail outright or take longer than they should can be traced to how they are conducted. People have a tendency to cut corners, underbudget, and assume that everything will somehow work out. They convince themselves that if they run into problems, they will be able to solve them. They assume that they have the support they need when they don't. They believe deeply that the changes they are undertaking are so important that everyone will understand the need for them and quickly get on board. They think of nothing but success, so they don't plan for the unexpected. They turn change over to consultants when they should stay more engaged themselves. They declare victory too soon, forgetting how hard sustaining change can be.

We know these things and yet we find it hard to avoid falling into the same traps again and again. Why? My belief is that it's because we are well intended but overwhelmed. We recognize the need for change and want to do it well, but there is too much going on to do everything we know we should do. We simply don't have the time or resources. Rather than ignore the need for change, we tell ourselves it's better to try even though we may not succeed. It is not that we intend to lead change poorly; it's that we don't have the tools we need to do a better job when there is too much change to handle.

What Makes Complex, Continuous Change Different?

The primary differences between complex, continuous change and single-change efforts is that triple-C demands prioritization, integration, not exceeding capacity, broader and deeper engagement, and agility.

Prioritization   Managing priorities across efforts involves decisions about such things as leadership attention, financial resources, stakeholder involvement, process changes, and organizational design. Although we can optimize these things for a single change, multiple changes require tradeoffs and, ultimately, suboptimization of one change to support other changes.

Integration   This involves integrating efforts to achieve the greatest impact in the shortest time at the least cost and with the least disruption. This requires seeing the big picture, understanding how efforts either reinforce or contradict one another, the impact that each effort will have on different parts of the system, and when and how everything will be accomplished. Attention to integration may mean that the timing or objectives of individual change efforts may actually shift in the context of other efforts under way. It also means making the effort to bring people together or otherwise keep them informed so that they understand how their work connects to that of others.

Not exceeding capacity   This requires understanding the capacity of the organization to manage change, not overloading the system with more simultaneous change than it can handle, and finding ways to increase change capacity to allow more change to occur concurrently. This involves identifying change bottlenecks, like the same people being assigned to multiple change projects they cannot fully support. It also involves managing the organization's emotional capacity; there is only so much change that people can tolerate before they become numb.

Complex, continuous change requires greater emotional investment than single-change efforts. People need to manage relationships up, down, and across that are shifting in their nature and intensity. They need to be executing plans and adjusting them at the same time. The energy required to manage all the change that is occurring while keeping customers satisfied may be greater than what is available. Organizations can reach the breaking point, as demonstrated by some of the cases covered earlier. As leaders of complex, continuous change, we need to have one foot on the gas and the other on the brake at the same time while constantly striving to improve the capacity of our organizations to change.

Broader and deeper engagement   By its very nature, triple-C requires tapping into collective intelligence to manage the complexity of everything that is happening instead of leaving integration to an individual or team, who quickly become overloaded with information or problems to solve.

Agility   Single changes sometimes require adjusting the approach based on what actually happens. Complex, continuous change always involves adjusting the approach and priorities on the fly as new information becomes available. While single changes can be "rolled out," continuous change is always "a work in progress." The nature of continuous change may cause the outcomes of earlier changes to be undone to allow progress against new objectives to be made.

Success at complex, continuous change requires more than initiating multiple single-change efforts and hoping that things will work out. We can't simply trust that overlaps will be resolved, the right resources will be available when needed, parts of the organization will not become overloaded, individuals won't burn out, changes will align rather than conflict, and so forth. This is a key point that must be emphasized because it is probably the single greatest threat to success in managing multiple changes simultaneously: *Complex, continuous change requires focus and integration beyond that involved in undertaking single-change efforts.* In the world of complex, continuous change, one plus one often equals zero unless the overall change is properly led.

Effective Change Leadership: What Does It Require?

This book is about the effective leadership of complex, continuous change. We need to know what to do when we can't slow things down to a manageable pace or pretend that one change does not affect another. Throughout this book are examples of companies that have faced enormous complex change challenges and succeeded and others that did not fare so well. The lessons of these examples form the foundation of the model presented in chapter 2, which shapes the structure of the remainder of the book.

If you are looking for a simple, one-sentence piece of advice from all that follows, it is *Step away from the buffet.* Our overwhelming need to respond to the threats and opportunities we face often forces us into immediate action that is not well conceived. We try to do too much at once without a coherent plan. We put so much on our plate that we cannot manage it all. We don't think about how multiple changes work against one another. We trust our intuition to guide our actions instead of stepping back to develop a better-informed plan of attack. We should not confuse activity with progress. Instead we should get on top of things, decide what's really important, and do those things well. If we want to succeed at complex, continuous change, we must use a rigorous approach. Although it is tempting and sometimes rewarding in the short run to jump into immediate action, that is not what successful leaders of complex, continuous change do. They use tools and methods that help them discover what's important, assess the current situation, undertake change more effectively, and learn from their experiences.

"Stepping away from the buffet" is not as easy as it might sound, but it is certainly doable. The more rigorous thinking you do, the more you will change the way you approach challenges and opportunities. As you will see, thinking more rigorously will require the adoption of specific tools, mindsets, and even structures that enable you to achieve repeatable success in leading complex, continuous change. If the changes you are facing are simple or occur one at a time, you probably don't need to read further. For better or worse, most of us need to improve how our organizations (and even we at a personal level) lead through complex, continuous change.

Leading complex, continuous change does not have to be like riding a roller coaster. You don't need to fear the sudden drop or wonder if you will survive. There will be twists and turns, to be certain. If you are a successful triple-C leader, you know this and plan for the unexpected to be a part of your day. You don't lead as if change is a single, onetime event, occurring in isolation from everything around it. Nor do you simply take the plunge and jump into change without really thinking about it.

As a successful change leader, you *pause* to discover what is really going on before you leap to the next change opportunity and then the next. You prepare for the work that is necessary to manage change as a complex, interpenetrating series of change processes. You *pause* to decide which of the many opportunities are the most important to do well. You make tough choices among attractive options because you know that trying to do everything is a recipe for failure. You *pause* to plan how you will go about change and who needs to be engaged for it to be done well and quickly. You push the envelope instead of playing it safe because you know that multiple changes are required, but you don't expect your approach to work as planned. Instead you monitor its progress and pay attention to the internal and external signals that tell you how things are going. You deal with the lack of readiness for change through deeper engagement and the creation of greater change capacity. You draw in key stakeholders whose support you need. Finally, you *pause* to reflect on what you have learned and put in place stronger processes and structures to help you do all of these things better in the future. You *pause* to see things in perspective, bringing people together frequently to make certain they are aligned. You don't divert your attention until you have either accomplished your objectives or reset your goals to address more-urgent needs. You *pause* to celebrate success but work even harder at capturing what you have learned because change won't stop and it won't get easier.

After a time you find that your organization's capacity to manage change has increased. You leverage the competitive advantage this provides to make it harder for others to catch up or, if you are a nonprofit, to intensify the impact of your work. You win and live to ride the Comet another day.

Leading Complex, Continuous Change

TO AVOID the sensation of riding a roller coaster when leading complex, continuous change, you need to take control. To do that, you need a plan, an approach that works.

The new CEO of a consumer products company took over after an extended period of mediocre performance. After some investigation he soon realized that there would be no quick or simple fix for the problems the organization was facing.

The company had been built by a series of acquisitions that had never been fully integrated. As a result, each unit ran independently, with few synergies being achieved. Furthermore, the culture of each unit was distinct, and people from one culture had little respect for the others. To add to the challenge, each unit was headed by a vice president who sought to maximize his autonomy, making it difficult to reach consensus on the changes necessary to improve performance. From an operations standpoint, each unit ran on its own IT platform and fiscal calendar, making integrated financial management a challenge. Each unit had its own salesforce, meaning the company sent multiple salespeople to call on the same customers, with different terms being offered. The supply chain was not integrated, and manufacturing costs and quality varied widely from one location to another.

Across the units, job titles and compensation levels were not uniform, causing perceptions of inequality and confusion about who should be included in meetings. Because the units were not co-located, coordination was expensive and the geographical distances between them reinforced their separate identities. Very few common processes existed for managing innovation, customer service, human resources (HR), and financial planning and tracking.

Finally, the senior team was not aligned on the nature of the issues facing the organization or what to do about them. The former CEO had let these and other issues persist. He had been supportive of individual change efforts but did not step back to prioritize them or look for ways to integrate them and multiply their effectiveness. His support was actually benign neglect. He hoped that the efforts of each unit would address the issues, and he believed the reports he received regarding the progress being achieved. In truth he was deluding himself. He was unable to see the situation objectively and had no clue where to begin to drain the swamp he was in. He was riding the Comet, not knowing where it would take him.

The new CEO was an experienced hand who had seen a lot over the course of his career and understood that real change required focus, commitment, and sometimes unpopular decisions. He owed no allegiance to anyone and brought in a new head of HR to act as his adviser as he began clearing the decks. He understood that some issues were more important than others. He knew that so long as the units maintained their unique cultures and identities, he could not solve the other problems.

He began by prioritizing the issues that needed to be addressed, beginning with structural changes and replacing key leaders who held on to the past, including two of the unit vice presidents. Once these actions were taken, under the guidance of a cross-unit team, he began reappointing leaders to positions outside their original fiefdoms, with responsibility for developing common processes that cut across the entire enterprise. Duplicate functions were combined, the supply chain was consolidated, costs were slashed, and new policies were adopted. With the change of structure came job leveling, so that position titles meant roughly the same responsibilities and pay. Bright stars were promoted to positions of authority, and those who could not support the new order were allowed to either remain in less responsible positions or move on to other companies. Energy increased dramatically, and a belief that the organization could actually win grew and began shaping behavior. Results improved, as did morale, and people who had thought of leaving decided to stay. The change was dramatic but required the better part of five years to fully implement. Over this period the new CEO was constantly challenged but never flinched. He stayed the course until the change had settled in and was irreversible before he retired.

A Model for Leading Complex, Continuous Change

We could look at the actions of the new CEO from a heroic perspective, attributing the success to his good judgment alone. Clearly, he deserved the credit for the change, whereas the former CEO would never have achieved the same results. Yet there was more to the story than his heroism. Many others provided expertise and commitment and stayed the course through the twists and turns. Without them the new CEO would have accomplished little. His expertise was in change leadership, not simply change management. He understood how to motivate people to change and how to guide them through the difficult emotional waters that dramatic change entails. He had the emotional intelligence and strength of values to deal with people respectfully but fairly. He did not tolerate dissension, and he rewarded those who took risks with their careers to support change for the better. He put the needs of the enterprise before his own comfort, trusting that the talented people he put on the change team would push him in ways that even he would find challenging. In all of this, with the help of his advisers, he followed an implicit approach to change that was built on many past experiences, learning from what worked and what did not.

The model he followed was not committed to paper then; it was still in its formative stages. How it has evolved is shown in figure 2.1.

The Actions

The key actions that must be taken to manage complex, continuous change are Discovering, Deciding, Doing, and Discerning. Unlike linear change models, these actions do not occur in sequence but rather simultaneously. The situation demands where attention should be placed at a given moment; but the art of leading complex, continuous change involves taking a "helicopter view" of what is happening and deciding which actions, or combinations of actions, will have the greatest impact. We discuss

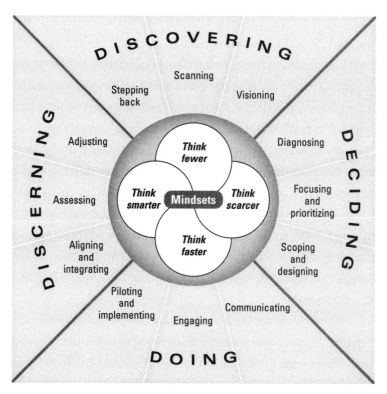

Figure 2.1 A Model for Leading Complex, Continuous Change

them one at a time, but this is not because there is a starting and ending place intended. Complex, continuous change is ongoing and defies a strictly linear approach to its management. In the following chapters, we go into each of the actions in greater detail.

Discovering: *stepping back, scanning, visioning* While change is a necessity, not all change is a necessity right now. Getting better at staying focused on what matters while stepping away from the buffet of possibilities is a process that few organizations have mastered. The fact is, there is a reality related to finite time and resources. We can increase the time and resources somewhat through the actions recommended in this book, but there are still limits. Doing everything, rather than some things, is a recipe for failure. Moreover, leading complex change requires a focus on the work of change, even in the face of distractions. Once momentum is lost, it is hard to regain.

The Discovering actions involve taking stock of the situation to determine what the overall direction of the sum of the change efforts under way should be. The primary focus here is on what is happening outside the organization rather than internally. The internal matchup of current capabilities against future demands takes place during the Deciding phase in the model but, as stated, both Discovering and Deciding may occur simultaneously.

The work of the Discovering stage has two other important benefits. First, it causes senior leaders to become more aligned with the overall direction of the company and the long-term objectives that must be accomplished. Second, it helps leaders formulate metrics, milestones, and timeframes for change that serve as the foundation for planning and taking stock of progress. Because change is often impeded by either a lack of alignment among senior leaders or confusion regarding the urgency of actions to be taken, these additional benefits of the Discovery process are significant.

Deciding: *diagnosing, focusing and prioritizing, scoping and designing* Your organization has a limit to how much change it can handle. Until you can build greater change capacity, you must try to avoid overloading the system with change because doing this will only slow you down and decrease your chances of success. To increase capacity, you first need to do some sleuthing. Who in your organization actually takes part in leading change, and how well do they do it? What more is needed to build greater change capacity into the organization so that it becomes easier rather than harder over time to keep up with the pace of change? Do you leverage the existing informal networks to speed up change and make change efforts more effective, or do you rely on the formal organization to do everything at the same time?

The Deciding phase is where guidance is developed that directs the work of change across the organization. The vision provides the overall direction for changes that will allow the organization to thrive in its competitive environment. The Deciding phase determines what about the organization must change internally to allow this to happen. Diagnosing the fit between the current state and the desired state helps us understand what is important to address. The work of focusing and prioritizing forces us to step away from the buffet of possible change activities to make certain that the activities we choose will address the most important issues. Finally, scoping and designing provides the roadmap for the change: who, when, where, and how.

Doing: *communicating, engaging, piloting and implementing*
Whatever your organization's current pace of change, it is probably too slow. Increasing the clock speed of change from start to finish usually requires a shift not just in processes but in how you think about change. You cannot continue to work as though you are living in a turn-of-the-last-century, steamship-travel, paper-mail world. We live in the digital age, but we lead and run our organizations the same way our ancestors did: slow, plodding decisions; disconnected actions; long feedback loops that lead

to slow course corrections; underfunded and underresourced efforts that compete with one another for time and attention; sending things up the hierarchy for approval. To keep up with the pace of change, get out of its way.

In complex, continuous change, executing is always happening. Helping people understand what to pay attention to and why at any given moment requires constant communication. Tapping the collective intelligence of the organization helps the overall change process be faster and more effective, as people lend their commitment and ideas to the effort. Gaining commitment and drawing out ideas takes more than communication; it takes engagement. Finally, implementing change is an art in itself, especially when a lot of it is happening simultaneously. Piloting using rapid prototyping saves enormous time and energy so that the careful work that leads to successful implementation can take place.

Discerning: *aligning and integrating, assessing, adjusting*   Discerning is about learning with a purpose; namely, to get better at responding effectively to complex, continuous change. To learn we need ways to know whether we are improving or getting worse, so this work begins with developing metrics. We need to be able to align and integrate across all that is happening so that we can see the trends that tell us what is going well and what is not. For example, have we cut the number of change projects under way at the same time by 50 percent? Are at least 75 percent of them on track? Do our employee engagement surveys show an improvement in people's confidence in our future or the ability of the executive team to lead change? Are we conducting rigorous after-action reviews to answer the questions *What did we expect* *to happen? What actually happened? Why?* and *What should we do differently the next time?*

Once we have collected data, the next step in Discerning is to make sense of it. This is best done by involving people who bring a fresh perspective to the table. Just as in Discovering, we need to be certain that there are people present who can challenge what we think we see, given our natural tendency to see what we expect to see.

Finally, we need to formulate some actions for the next time we undertake change. What will we do better the next time, and how will we know whether it helped?

In single-change efforts, learning is a low priority because the change may not be repeated. In complex, continuous change, learning is a wise investment. To learn, we must discern what is working as intended and what is not. Aligning and integrating change efforts requires real-time learning. Assessing what is being accomplished compared with what was expected requires reflection. Finally, the whole point of learning is to adjust actions going forward so that more can be accomplished with less.

The four actions are in constant interplay with one another as complex, continuous change plays out. There is no starting or ending point and no annual calendar that guides when one action should be the focus over another. The four actions must be simultaneous. How is this possible? The answer lies in *how* the four actions are carried out.

We have been accustomed to thinking of any project, including a change project, as a series of steps to be completed one at a time. We may have such a strong commitment to the one-step-at-a-time mindset that we may think, like one CEO I spoke with recently, that there is no way to undertake more than one of the four actions at once. Like when we solve a brainteaser, we have to relax our assumptions and think outside the lines to solve the problem. Here's how.

Taking Action

As we begin the process of Discovering, who is in the room? Do we envision the senior team around the table? Or can we imagine a room or series of rooms in which many people are helping us Discover? While they are helping us Discover, are they paying attention to what is already going on? Are they thinking about how important the new concepts are compared with what is already under way? If so, they are also engaged in the process of Deciding. At the same time, isn't their knowledge of how difficult certain changes will be to make entering their thinking? Are they imagining the difficulties they will encounter and what to do about them? If so, they are already planning and preparing for Doing. If they report out what they are finding, they are helping others understand what is under consideration and why, which is both Doing and a little bit of Discerning, especially if they are leveraging what they learned from failing to communicate early on the last time.

There are certainly times when one of the four actions is the primary focus. Nevertheless, the challenge of leading complex, continuous change requires that we avoid becoming trapped in a "step" without moving forward, backward, and sideways among Discovering, Deciding, Doing, and Discerning.

In reality, the experience of leading complex, continuous change is anything but orderly, as indicated in figure 2.2. Faced with the challenge of complex, continuous change, putting

Figure 2.2 Complex, Continuous Change as Actually Experienced

together a Gantt chart would be futile, as it would change before the ink was dry.

The four actions and mindsets at the core of the model for complex, continuous change are shown in figure 2.3.

Although it is easy to read figure 2.3 left to right, again, in reality, the four actions are always occurring simultaneously, which is what makes complex, continuous change so challenging. While the objectives of each action are distinct, as are the processes used to accomplish them, what is important is that *all*

	Discovering	Deciding	Doing	Discerning
Actions				
Objectives	Identify viable opportunities and vision; revise as required	Prioritize efforts to close the gap between the vision and current reality	Engage the organization in executing the change strategy	Learn from experience to improve change capacity over time
Mindsets	*Think fewer*	*Think scarcer*	*Think faster*	*Think smarter*

Figure 2.3 The Four Actions and Mindsets

four actions are done well, as an integrated whole. We talk about each of the actions in greater detail in the following chapters.

Finally, the words at the bottom of each column in figure 2.3 should be turned into posters and displayed prominently wherever complex changes are being discussed. They remind us what we should be thinking when things get challenging.

The Mindsets Required

Change challenges come in different sizes and intensities. Nevertheless I cannot recall a change leader complaining about there not being enough need for change or having too much time or too many resources to effect the change. I also don't recall one saying that people were working together too well or that internal and external stakeholders were doing a lot more than they were asked. What does this suggest? *(1) That we are often surprised by the amount of change we must undertake and (2) that we have not always adopted the mindsets we need to lead complex, continuous change.*

Change leaders who try to take on more change than they can really handle are like pilots with too heavy a load and too short a runway. When the airplane does not lift off and the end of the runway is approaching, they pull back on the yoke to try to force the airplane to fly. Instead of climbing, the pilot soon discovers that there is insufficient power to overcome the laws of aerodynamics; airspeed declines rapidly, the airplane stalls, and then it crashes. If the pilot wants to take off successfully, the choices are to unload some weight, find a longer runway, or equip the plane with more power and a combination of wings and flaps that allow a steeper climb. Once you're in an overloaded airplane and have used up the available runway, it's too late to start over.

If you agree that it is time to address this situation in your organization, here are the four mindsets you will need to support the four actions in the model for complex, continuous change.

Think fewer   Behind every aspiration to improve is real work. We sometimes forget that when we are told we should "think big" or "aim high." There's nothing wrong with aspiring to be better. There would be no reason to engage in strategic thinking if your intent is to stay the same. We should all force ourselves to strive for improvements that are on the very edge of our ability to achieve. At the same time, if our vision calls for us to save the world, we must understand what's involved and come to our senses about what's realistically possible. Saving the world, becoming number one in our industry, and being the recognized leader in customer service are admirable goals but often involve more work and require more investments and commitments than we are actually prepared to make.

Stakeholders and employees lose confidence in leaders who are overly optimistic. Setting lofty goals that you cannot possibly achieve without tying them to specific things you are committed to do opens the door to people's undertaking too many unaligned, overly costly efforts that in the end produce frustration rather than progress.

Thinking fewer means thinking realistically and thoroughly about what you are asking people to do. Do not set so many goals that they cannot possibly be achieved. The vision you set forth should be attainable, and the way you are going to get there should involve a manageable number of things that you are deeply committed to do. Do not simply dream big, fling open the doors, and wait for the deluge of ideas to come rushing in. Starting with a few clear and very important aspirations will reduce the chances that you will be completely overwhelmed by complex, continuous change.

Finally, just a note on what Jim Collins and Jerry Porras called "Big Hairy Audacious Goals," or "BHAGs," in their book *Built to Last.*[1] Does "thinking fewer" mean we should give up big dreams? After all, aren't we living in the age of "If we build it, they will come" and "If we can think it, we can do it"? My view is that audacious goals are more important than ever. Not having them, as Collins and Porras found, is why many companies fail. The point of thinking fewer is to *focus,* not to give up on what is both important and exciting. Pick one or two big goals and go for them, but don't try to do everything you can imagine at the same time. By thinking fewer there is a *better* chance that a few big changes will actually happen.

Think scarcer   You've heard it from Stephen Covey; you've heard it from time management experts; you've heard it from your financial adviser.² You can do almost anything you set your mind to, but you cannot do everything. Even with a tightly defined vision and a few clear goals, there is still much that needs to be done to achieve a transformation in your capabilities. I have worked with organizations that can list literally hundreds of projects that are under way simultaneously to achieve their vision. While this shows a real interest in making things better, it's not a recipe for success. Why? First, because there are not enough resources, time, and attention to do them all. Second, because many of the changes are interdependent, they need to be aligned with one another or they will work against each other in the end. Aligning efforts takes more time and resources; and the more changes there are to align, the greater the work and complexity involved. Finally, this book is about navigating churn in the real world. In the real world, more change is always right around the corner. Some of it can't be ignored. If your organization is already overdosing on change, you won't be able to respond to the new threats and opportunities that are always presenting themselves. You need to keep some energy in reserve. Think of the people, dollars, time, and energy you have to spend on change as scarce resources. Don't spend them without thinking carefully first. Get better at prioritizing.

But, you might ask, don't we live in a world of abundance? Isn't it true that if we dream, we will find a way? I really want to believe this, and I do believe that our aspirations shape our future reality. If we don't aspire to improve, we will never develop the capacity to do so. Please don't hear me saying that you should not dream or try to do more than you currently know how to do.

But here's the thing: you need a regular reality check. Navigating churn in the real world means that there are consequences if we don't meet our targets or we overspend our budgets or burn out our people. Certainly, try to do as much as you can as fast as you can and challenge yourself to invent new solutions that you have not tried before. But stop to assess your progress and make tough decisions about how much you can take on, for now. Keep Discovering and Discerning constantly so that you are continuously aware of the choices you are making about where to focus and what to prioritize. Don't keep chasing rainbows that are no longer as important or relevant as other things you should be doing.

Think faster   Develop a real hunger for speed. Question why things have to take as long as they do. Settle for a rapid prototype that can help you learn quickly rather than waiting for the perfect, complete, and polished solution. Appoint clear leadership instead of leaving responsibilities murky and trusting that people will figure out their roles. Examine how you undertake change projects to see where all the time goes. The real world demands that we respond to change at the pace that it is occurring, not on our own schedule of when it's most convenient.

Thinking faster often involves changing the way we do things. We cannot do something faster if the people we need to do it are already jammed up. But aren't there other people we could involve, even outside the organization if necessary? If we're already at capacity and need to move even faster, we need to think outside the box—or go back to thinking scarcer or fewer. In moving faster we cannot just add more to the queue; we have to make decisions to either do things differently or jettison some work. In the world of continuous change, putting things off until next year means starting out next year already behind, at a time when new changes need to be considered. Once you allow yourself to fall behind, you can never catch up.

Move quickly and move on—when it makes sense to do so. Shed the baggage you don't need if it's slowing you down and it's not essential. At the same time, keep investing in things that remain important and relevant, even if it takes time to achieve them.

Think smarter   Learning as you go is the mindset that allows you to grow change capacity over time. Because the world is not going to slow down or demand less change anytime soon, invest in developing your ability to take on more change efficiently and effectively. As you employ the other mindsets, you will see the effects they produce and understand more about how to apply them to improve both the rate of change and the amount of change you can handle. Whether projects succeed or fail, never miss an opportunity to learn from them what worked well and what caused problems. Develop ways of educating yourself and others about these things so that each time you formulate a new vision, decide priorities, look for faster ways to do things, and assess what happened, you do it better and smarter.

Yes, thinking smarter takes time and adds costs. Thinking smarter falls into the category of things you need to do to "slow down to speed up." Taking the time and making the effort to learn is an investment that will repay itself as soon as you undertake your next change effort and avoid the pitfalls of the last.

Note that we are speaking about leadership mindsets here and that "leadership" can be plural as well as singular. It is not that one person must be able to do these things but that leadership as a body has these shared mindsets. In facing complex, continuous change, an organization will go no faster or farther than its leaders' mindsets will take it. When the amount of change required outpaces these mindsets, the ride on the Comet begins. After discussing the actions involved in undertaking continuous change, we'll return to look more closely at how these mindsets can be nurtured.

Discovering: Think Fewer

THE OBJECTIVE of Discovering is to identify viable opportunities for change. Later, having identified these opportunities, decisions can be made about which ones to pursue. During Discovering, it is important to remember to *think fewer* because the attraction to do everything that is discovered leads to overloads that can prove to be unmanageable. The goal is to identify the most important opportunities rather than create an exhaustive list.

Leading complex, continuous change involves stepping back, scanning the internal and external environment, and, from what is found, either developing or recrafting a vision that aligns people with the desired direction. Pitfalls in this activity include relying exclusively on internal perspectives, letting the past blind views of future possibilities, and falling in love with too many ideas.

There are three key subcomponents of Discovering:

▶ Stepping back: calling a time-out to do a thorough appraisal of possibilities

▶ Scanning: collecting valid information about the current state of affairs

▶ Visioning: creating a clear picture of the desired future

The quality of the opportunities that are identified in Discovering sets the upper limit on the impact that change efforts can have. Do Discovering well, and there will be huge possibilities to change things in a dramatic fashion. Do it poorly, and almost nothing that follows will be worth the time and effort. What does doing Discovering well require? A rigorous approach that combines the right team using the right process, collecting the right data, and reaching the right conclusions.

The right team   The Discovering team should ideally comprise seven to nine people and include representatives from top leadership as well as from other levels, units, and functions of the organization. Together they should include members who are capable of thinking strategically, represent the customer's point of view, bring an objective perspective, know how to communicate, and can make sense of complex data. They should have instant credibility in the eyes of others both within and outside the organization. Finally, they should be team players who place the good of the organization above their own interests.

To keep things fresh, the team should shift membership over time but not all at the same time. Memory of the team's history is an important input but shouldn't be the reason to avoid rethinking decisions that were made by previous configurations of the team.

The right process   When the team meets, it should follow guidelines that help optimize its work. This begins with setting aside enough time to do a good job of collecting information, analyzing data, and making decisions. Experience suggests that this can be 10 percent or more of each person's time for the period over which the team is in existence, whether it meets on a regular basis or compresses the work into several longer sessions.

During the time the team is meeting, it needs to ensure that there is frequent communication with the organization so that the team's work is transparent to others. This helps others feel included and makes their expertise available to the process.

Team meetings need to be well planned and well run. Teams should develop guidelines regarding scheduling, participation, attendance, decision making, communication, leadership, and facilitation. Each moment together is precious, so time should not be wasted.

The right data   To understand what is going on inside and outside the organization in order to know which changes to consider, the team should undertake a thorough and objective 360-degree assessment of the situation. This assessment should consider internal data such as financial measures, employee engagement, turnover, quality, safety, and change projects currently under way. External data should include measures of customer satisfaction, competitiveness, shareholder value created, compliance, risk, and market conditions.

Data should be forward looking, including potential scenarios and capabilities that will be required to respond to emerging trends. Data should also include a historical look at strengths and weaknesses.

Obviously, each team and each organization will need to decide how much of what kinds of data to collect before arriving at the saturation point where nothing new is being learned. Teams also vary in how much they want to be involved in collecting data themselves rather than relying on data that are readily available. While there are no hard-and-fast rules regarding the right amount of data to collect, teams should remember that Discovery is not done once but rather on an ongoing basis. Complex, continuous change requires that we strive to learn more as new data become available. We don't have to know everything before we move on to Deciding. In fact, we never will know *everything*. We just need to know enough to make the best decisions we can for the moment.

The right conclusions   There is a difference between data and insight. Simply collecting information is not the goal of Discovering. The real goal is to understand what is happening inside and outside the organization so that we can make the best decisions possible about when and where to invest in change. The outputs of the team's work should include a reduced set of changes to be considered, a rough estimate of the time and resources required to address them, the outcomes that making the changes should produce, and greater clarity about what needs to change *now* and what can remain the same for the time being.

What can *never* work is to have the same team that created the current strategic plan assess the need to redirect resources toward new opportunities, using the same assumptions they used before. Something should be done differently in Discovering to generate new ideas and directions. Clayton Christensen's book *The Innovator's Dilemma* lays out the reasons why.[1] Essentially, if you use the strategy team to do Discovering work, the team will blind itself to data that don't fit what they thought they would see, even if the external context has changed. To lead complex, continuous change, you need a team that is capable of discovering anew the opportunities that should be considered. Here is a look at each of the three subcomponents of the Discovering process in greater detail.

Stepping Back
Committing to the Right Team and the Right Process

Stepping back properly requires that you call a time-out to do some quality thinking. Ronald Heifetz, in *Leadership without Easy Answers,* talks about "getting on the balcony," where you can see all the action that is taking place below you.[2] If you are on the dance floor, he says, things look very confusing; but from above, you can begin to see the patterns that are causing the chaos below. For leaders, *getting on the balcony* means removing themselves from the day-to-day entanglements that come with putting out fires so as to have the time to think strategically. With fires constantly burning and new ones breaking out every day, it is extremely difficult to call a time-out. Yet failing to do so condemns us to expend our energy in the service of putting out small fires instead of getting the larger blaze under control. Although the top team may see this as their work, two things argue against their doing it themselves: they don't have the time to do the work well, and they cannot be objective about what they find. Better that they commission others to undertake the Discovering task and reserve their own time and energy to review the inputs and make decisions about the next actions to be taken: Deciding, Doing, and Discerning.

Consider the case of Lucent Technologies, the spinoff of AT&T's network systems and hardware business into a free-standing entity made necessary by the mandated breakup of the Bell system to promote competition. Employees who were part of Lucent were worried that their organization could not survive without the halo of the AT&T brand. Henry Schacht, a board member who was tapped to be acting CEO during the spinout, recognized their concerns. Instead of sharing dry business projections, Schacht responded by going on the road to talk to employees about what he perceived to be "the opportunity of a lifetime." As it turned out, he was right—at least for a while.

Freed from its connections with AT&T, Lucent's sales to former AT&T competitors took off. Its network systems unit, which supplied the huge mechanical switches that routed calls from one caller to another, was its growth engine. As a result, even leaders several levels down became millionaires overnight. After a couple of amazing years, Schacht turned over the reins of the company to CEO Richard McGinn, who no doubt must have felt like he was in exactly the right place at the right time.

Then two things happened. First, the pent-up demand for mechanical switches was quickly satiated. In addition, mechanical switches gradually became obsolete, replaced by smaller, less costly, and more reliable digital switching systems. Lucent's Bell Labs had been instrumental in inventing the digital switching system, but the company held off introducing it because mechanical switches were such an important source of revenue. As sales of mechanical switches fell, so did profits. In just a few years, Lucent went from being the darling of Wall Street to losing its footing and being acquired by its European competitor, Alcatel.

There is a lot more to the Lucent story, of course; there always is. Still, the question is, Why didn't Lucent have a better handle on its market? Why didn't its leaders get on the balcony, as Heifetz suggests, to see what was happening and adapt?

Contrast Lucent's story with that of Wilh. Wilhelmsen, a 160-year-old Norwegian shipping company that in the late 1990s was about to gasp its last breath. The container-shipping market had become hypercompetitive, with other companies slashing prices to steal market share. A series of decisions led Wilhelmsen to exit container shipping in favor of concentrating its remaining resources in oil-rig supply shipping; when oil prices suddenly dropped and oil rigs were shut down, Wilhelmsen was left high and dry. Facing bankruptcy, its leaders, to their credit, saw an opportunity to redirect the company away from its current strategy toward shipping automobiles and heavy equipment. Before this strategy could be fully implemented, however, tragedy struck; on the way to christen a new ship, the entire executive team and half the headquarters staff perished in a plane crash. After a long period of mourning, the company's new leadership eventually drove the company forward, until it became the largest player in the space it had created, growing its fleet from nine to 177 ships.

Was this success due to the replacement of the former leadership team by a completely new one? Possibly, but there is evidence that the former team was already moving in the right direction. When forced to do so by market realities, they were able to get on the balcony and figure out what needed to change. They could have easily given up, sold the remaining assets, and walked away, but they cared enough about the company to want it to continue, and they weren't afraid to try.

The leaders I have worked with who are best at considering new opportunities ask themselves, *What would investors like KKR and Carl Icahn do if they were to acquire us tomorrow?* By this I mean that they don't allow themselves the luxury of standing pat. They don't simply assume that they can continue being successful by doing what they are doing or being organized as they are currently organized. If Icahn would break the company into pieces to make each one more focused and the sum total more valuable, why should the leaders wait for him to force them to do so rather than just do it themselves? Basically, it means taking an external perspective rather than allowing the organization to become complacent. So, you don't need to wait for KKR or Icahn to come knocking at the door; my belief is that you don't need to bring in a new CEO or a whole new leadership team to manage complex, continuous change more effectively—unless the old team is not willing to do it.

To set up the Discovering process, the senior team should select one or two of its members to sponsor the process and be directly engaged in it, along with the team that is recruited to do the heavy lifting of the Discovering work. Without direct top-level engagement, the team will find it difficult to successfully challenge existing commitments. Experience indicates that without direct representation, it is sometimes difficult to convince the senior team that significant change should occur. Involving representatives from the senior team greatly increases the chances of a fair hearing for challenging suggestions.

In constructing the team, it is important to pay attention to both internal and external credibility. To the extent that the team's recommendations demand changes in strategy, focus, organizational arrangements, or work processes, stakeholders inside and outside the organization will need to be brought into alignment. This is much easier when they respect the members of the team doing the Discovering work.

During their work, the team will find it necessary to alternate between collecting information, analyzing it, and communicating its findings to various constituencies, always after first reviewing the work with the senior team. Seeding the team with people who possess the capabilities to do these tasks well tips the balance in favor of efficiency and success.

Because change is continuous, stepping back is a periodic, ongoing activity rather than a onetime affair. To keep the process fresh, members should rotate on and off the team in a way that preserves some continuity while allowing new members to add different perspectives. Serving on this type of team has proven to be a great developmental experience for people with high potential—a side benefit that should not be ignored.

Once the team is formed, careful attention to creating a team charter, clarifying expectations, and then negotiating the team's mission with the senior team lays the foundation for productive effort. Once the process becomes routine, the senior team will become comfortable with the challenges posed by the Discovering team and even look forward to their exchanges. Both the senior team and the Discovering team will become more adept at their roles in the proceedings.

Discovering must keep pace with changes that are happening in the world. As noted previously, the concept of an annual strategy process is giving way to more-frequent check-ins. It makes little sense to continue with strategies that have fallen out of step with reality.

What does it mean to Discover differently in the face of complex, continuous change? Take the example of Lego, the toy block maker, discussed by Krupp and Schoemaker in *Winning the Long Game.* For a long time, Lego's market niche was secure and the future predictable. But then, like many of the stories of organizations facing complex change, Lego's world was turned upside down, seemingly overnight. Lower-priced foreign competition entered the market with identical products. At the same time, the tastes of children began to shift toward digital and online games. Blocks were not nearly as exciting as they once were. After 15 years of double-digit growth between 1980 and 1995, losses began to mount. Opportunities to partner with Lucasfilm were initially missed as internal solutions to the problem were sought.

One can only imagine the early discussions at Lego. How could this be happening? Years of complacency and easy growth were replaced with the need to figure out new answers—fast. Many leadership teams believe they are doing all they should with regard to Discovery, but Lego's leaders realize they have not done enough. What do Krupp and Schoemaker recommend?

First, they suggest identifying "weak signals" at the edge of your business model that could lead to change. What are new competitors up to? Using scenario analysis, project yourself into the future: what will be different in your industry? But don't stop there. Attend conferences and meetings that will expose you to new ideas you hadn't considered. Use personal and social networks to raise questions and seek creative suggestions. Read more widely and expose yourself to topics that you would not normally consider. The bottom line is to *get out there*—talk to customers, analysts, business leaders, academics, and others who might provide clues.

If your weekly executive meeting is 90 percent financial reviews, you're probably in trouble. Here is a rule of thumb to consider: *10-10-5*. That is, the top 10 percent of leaders in your organization should spend at least 10 percent of their time focused on five or more years in the future. It is not a huge commitment; it's the equivalent of a day every other week. If the top 10 percent of your leaders are not taking this small amount of time to do rigorous Discovering, who will? Lego is inventing new strategies, including making movies. So far, the news is encouraging. Old dogs *can* learn new tricks, but you have to make the effort.

Scanning

The Data Are Always Friendly

There is a saying among researchers that *The data are always friendly.* What this means is that researchers should not be discouraged if their initial hypotheses are disconfirmed. The purpose of research is to produce truth, not simply to affirm our beliefs. When data disconfirm what we thought to be true, something deeper and more meaningful is revealed. We are forced to ask more questions to understand what is happening and then to test our new hypotheses once again. Thomas Edison is famous for pointing out how much effort he put into learning what did *not* work before understanding what did.

In organizational settings, we are not held to research standards. We are allowed to invest in "experiments" (strategies) based on "hypotheses" (intuitive guesses) that are never really tested in a scientific sense. We may or may not achieve the results we hope for, but there are often many competing explanations for why things turn out as they do (competitors, the economy, currency fluctuations, even the weather). Rarely are we forced to admit that our hypotheses may have been incorrect.

The goal of effective scanning is to use data to challenge our views of what is possible and what is important. Scanning is not really hypothesis testing; it is more like rigorous hypothesis formation. Before we engage the organization in a course of action, or continue to invest in a strategy that may no longer be as relevant as it once was, we need to do a careful appraisal of the situation. That is what scanning provides when it is done well. What does doing scanning well entail?

Design thinkers at IDEO and Continuum understand that they cannot rely on their own creativity to achieve new product breakthroughs. They must follow rigorous processes that bring them into contact with consumers and force them to look at things from the consumer's point of view. Bringing together a diverse team of thinkers from different backgrounds and ensuring that each person's voice carries influence are other aspects of the design process that matter.

Contrast this with a worst-case scenario of a top-leadership team discussion of change. Social roles are well defined, as is the pecking order. People know from experience what ideas will be supported and which ones are likely to be shot down. Even before the conversation begins, the range of possibilities has been narrowed significantly. People want to look into the cause of issues but often find themselves discounting what they find or continuing to hope that existing solutions will eventually work. The leadership team may invite outsiders into conversations, but it's normally to give brief presentations rather than to stay and push for new resolutions. As a result of these defense mechanisms, leaders conclude that change is not necessary. Don't allow this scenario to become your reality!

If we shield ourselves from the truth, we will find that our later decisions cause our organizations to diverge further from the proper course. Eventually, the divergence will become too great to ignore, but by then returning to the right course may be difficult. In contrast, if we are effective in stepping back and scanning our environment, we make certain we talk to stakeholders who challenge our thinking, analysts who are critical, board members who advocate different strategies, community members who feel that the organization is not doing enough, customers who have been lost, employees who have left, and industry experts who see trends we have ignored. Capturing and keeping this information in the forefront during the scanning process can help in setting directions that are better informed, more comprehensive, and more robust.

How the data are collected matters. Once again it is tempting to look in convenient places for information that is easy to acquire but says very little that is new or challenging. To disprove existing hypotheses and point to new breakthroughs, you must look in places you haven't looked before or use methods that will yield new clues. That's why it's so important that design thinking firms like IDEO follow their methodology religiously. Getting out and spending time observing customers engaged in real activities almost always reveals surprises. Things you thought were important to customers are not, whereas things you thought didn't matter are of extreme importance. In a video recording of a customer who just purchased a cell phone, for example, the thick plastic casing around the product that is intended as a theft deterrent in the store turns out to be a customer deterrent when the product is brought home. As the increasingly frustrated customer struggles to cut through the plastic without causing bodily harm, you wonder if anyone raised his hand in the packaging-design meeting to ask, "Did we intend to make our customers hate us?"

The point is that the scanning team cannot just do a mindless scavenger hunt for data to complete their report. They have to get out of the room, talk with people, observe what's going on, and *understand* what the data mean. They must follow a rigorous process. They need to talk to people with contrary and unique points of view. They need to seek out the wisdom of objective experts. They need to be in the *learning* mode versus the *knowing* mode or they will miss important clues. They need to find disconfirming data rather than seek more evidence with a confirmation bias. Consumer research firms understand that it's not the *quantity* of data they collect that matters but rather the *quality* of insights they gain in the process. How can teams test the quality of their scanning? By answering questions like these:

▶ How certain are we that what we have found represents the reality of what is happening versus what we want to see (minimal bias)?

▶ Are we able to compare what is happening with what has happened in the past and what others like us are experiencing (comparability)?

▶ Are we reasonably certain that we aren't missing anything that is important (completeness)?

▶ If others were to look at our situation, would they see the same things (perception)?

▶ Have we faithfully represented the viewpoints of different stakeholder groups (perspective)?

Do not confuse activity with value. To add real value, the data we collect must be valid, and their meaning must be derived through a series of carefully constructed conversations. The payoff from rigorous scanning is the derivation of key conclusions that explain what is taking place but also point to areas that may require further change.

If you want to benchmark your ability to scan and react, learn the story of Nokia, but be prepared—it's not a happy ending. Few firms in history have gone through the transformations that Nokia has since its founding in 1865. Here is a brief chronology of the shifts that occurred:

▶ 1865: Founded as a paper mill

▶ 1920s: Merged with a rubber manufacturer to make boots, tires, and rubber bands

▶ 1940s: Merged again to focus on power and telephone cables

▶ 1960s: Began semiconductor research

▶ 1970s: Developed digital telephone switching systems (remember Lucent?)

▶ 1980s: Entered mobile phones and built the world's first cellular network

▶ 1990s: Created GSM (Global System for Mobile Communications) networks and added televisions

▶ 1992: Downturn led to focus on telecom and divestiture of all other businesses

▶ 2010s: Further decline led to purchase of phone business by Microsoft, leaving only mapping services, network infrastructure, and advanced solutions

So, from 1865 through 1990 Nokia was an amazing company. Few organizations are as willing to step away from their roots and explore truly new territories. Imagine the organizational changes that needed to occur to enable these shifts. How did leaders who grew up in the paper or rubber business feel about the new strategies? What data convinced them that growth would necessitate fundamental shifts in products and strategies that would leave them behind as others stepped forward? Why were Nokia leaders able to listen while other companies discounted the need to change and went out of business? We should all consider the answers to these questions.

Then something happened at Nokia. The need to continue to evolve seemed to dissipate. Could it be that becoming number one in the mobile phone space made it too hard to step away from the business, even when losses and layoffs were mounting? Did Nokia leaders stop scanning the business environment to understand what was happening? Were they open to the voices of people who challenged the wisdom of continuing to invest in the mobile phone strategy? Or, did senior management meetings resemble the worst-case scenario described earlier in this chapter? We don't know, but *something* changed and not for the better. The answers to these questions are also something we should all consider.

It is possible that leaders at Nokia or Lucent could have seen what was coming more clearly had they employed the approach to scanning outlined here. It's just as likely that nothing could have prevented their fall because their investment in their core businesses was simply too great. I liken this to an *all-in* situation in gambling: After sustaining a long series of losses believing you can win, you're left with so little money that your only strategy is to go all-in to try to win back enough resources to continue the game. If you lose, you're out. Scanning is most useful when you still have enough resources to consider the options it uncovers. If you wait until you have to go all-in, there's a chance you might still win but an equal or greater chance that you will be out of the game.

If for some reason the Discovering team approach to scanning does not appeal to you, there are alternatives. I have worked with senior teams who see Discovering as *their* work and are eager to engage in it themselves. That is a viable option if the team can spare the time needed to do the work well and are clear that they need to bring in outside voices that will disrupt their current thinking. It seems that most executive teams love an interesting and well-informed presentation. The caveat, as noted earlier, is that the team cannot simply dismiss what was presented once the presenter is gone. Therefore, if the senior team chooses to do the work, it makes sense that the process be facilitated by someone whose role is to maintain the integrity of the dialogue and overall rigor of the process.

Another option is to outsource the scanning process to a strategy consulting firm. The pro of this approach is that consulting firms do a lot of this kind of work. They don't need to start from scratch, they have ready benchmarks, and they can be objective in assessing the need for change. The con is that they do not always generate deep commitment to the changes they recommend. Outside experts may not understand the cultural or political nuances at play among internal and external stakeholders. The senior team may not agree with the consultant's conclusions because members of the senior team were not directly involved and may not fully understand why the recommendations were made. Even if the senior team accepts the recommendations, execution efforts may be halfhearted because there wasn't true buy-in to begin with. Finally, the deep knowledge gained by direct exposure to others during the scanning process will stay with the consulting firm rather than the organization.

A fourth approach is to do what Marvin Weisbord in *Productive Workplaces* calls, "getting the whole system in the room."[3] Under Samuel Palmisano, IBM initiated online "Jams" with hundreds of thousands of employees to get their input on the company's mission. The opportunity to contribute was no doubt gratifying and appreciated but probably left people wondering who was going to read all the comments and how much their individual voices would matter.

A hybrid of these approaches is possible but makes the work complex and the outputs difficult to integrate into a coherent picture that leads to a focused plan of action. Organizations may wish to experiment with different methods until they find an approach that seems right to them.

Visioning
Vision as Touchstone

The word *touchstone* comes from a type of black rock that was used to test the purity of gold or silver samples as the samples were rubbed on the rock. The vision serves as a touchstone for all actions to follow. Visioning and re-visioning are important in a constantly changing world. With regard to change, the vision serves as a touchstone as actions are "rubbed" against the vision to see if they are consistent or inconsistent with the direction that has been set. In a world of complex, continuous change, the vision should be updated to reflect significant developments. In that way it remains a valuable touchstone for the assessment of current allocations of time and effort.

Generic visions are of little use in leading complex, continuous change. *To be number one in the world* conveys an aspiration without suitable guidance to direct prioritization decisions and their associated actions to follow. When, in the early 1990s, Arthur Martinez declared to a meeting of several hundred of his top leaders that Sears would become a leader in customer focus, it must have taken a tremendous amount of courage for a lone one of those present to raise his hand to say that he wasn't certain what Martinez meant; he thought he already was customer-focused and wasn't certain what more he should do. As it turned out, no one really understood what customers wanted from their experience of shopping at Sears, and it took another year's effort to collect information from customers to begin to clarify the answer. Rather than stating, "We will become more customer focused," perhaps a more meaningful vision at the time would have been "We will learn about our customers so that we can provide the products, services, and experiences they desire from Sears." The first statement could release a barrage of change initiatives from the profoundly important to the inanely absurd, and no one would be able to tell the difference. The second would direct activity to a more narrow focus—namely, to actions that would lead to a deeper understanding of customer desires.

Visions determine the size of the funnel that will be used to capture opportunities for change. Too broad a vision results in too large a funnel, swamping the organization with change initiatives that are competing, underresourced, cross-contaminating, and ultimately overwhelming. In this way the broad vision, intended to inspire, ends up frustrating progress.

"Thinking fewer" in the Discovering phase means that we need to give more-precise direction through our visions, with the full understanding that the vision will no doubt change in the face of what actually takes place within and beyond the organization during the next period of time. Broad visions, which seem less likely to need adjustment (*Be number one in the world!*), are likely to retard real change instead of advance it. More-precise but temporary visions help people move from inaction to action, knowing that what they do is aligned with what is needed in the moment. Clear visions are like previews of the roller-coaster ride: it may still be a challenge, but at least you know what you are getting into!

How do you create a focused but still compelling vision that aligns people and motivates action? This is ultimately the responsibility of the senior team, with assistance from others as required. The attributes we are seeking in the vision are the following.

Make me believe   The vision creates a gap between current ways of operating and what will be required that initiates a call to action. It explains what will be different and why the vision is important in terms of the advantages it provides to both the organization and individual stakeholders. It makes the future attractive because it ties into the emotions of those taking part in the journey, meets the organization's need for sustainability, and provides opportunities for growth, learning, and a better quality of life for stakeholders. It also connects to history and current strengths so that the step forward builds on the past and seems achievable. The vision must not be generic; rather, it should resonate with people in its uniqueness and appropriateness to this organization rather than any other.

Don't focus on problems   While I won't go into detail here, there is evidence from recent research by Gervase Bushe and Neelima Paranjpey indicating that changes intended to solve problems are not nearly as successful as changes aimed at inventing new ways of doing things.[4] Visions should motivate people to think differently, invent new ways of doing things, and generally lead to a better future, not just correct deficiencies or take us back to "the good old days." Engage people's minds as well as their hearts. Problems provoke negative emotions and a desire to escape the situation, whereas a challenge to devise a better process or a better future engages people, resulting in increased energy and creativity.

Tell me how   The vision should help guide shorter-term actions that will move the organization toward the longer-term ideal state. It should outline at a very high level what will be required to achieve the vision. Often it includes specific challenges the organization must address or things that must change to make the vision a reality. There is no specific plan at this stage but rather just enough focus to narrow the efforts and keep them aligned—what is in and out of bounds.

Make it personal   The vision should personalize the message. It should convey our personal excitement and commitment as well as help people understand not only what's in it for them but what they are expected to contribute. To motivate action, the vision must help people see their part in realizing the vision rather than be something that they will "experience" as others do the work and deliver the future to them.

Make it urgent   Do not bother talking about a vision that you have no intention of working toward for months or years. Talk to people when the time for action is *now*, then repeat the message continuously so that people know it is urgent. Track progress and find ways to make progress visible for all to see. Use small wins as opportunities to applaud actions. Keep reminding people what is next and what comes after that.

Make it real   While the vision may need to change over time as you learn from experience or face new challenges, it is not okay for key people to "wait and see" what happens or to speak against the vision. Deal with prominent leaders whose actions are not aligned with the vision. Invite other resistors into discussions to understand their concerns. Make adjustments if necessary, but do not back down on the overall direction. People watch for cracks in the facade. Don't allow them.

Make it truthful   Do not oversell the benefits or pretend that you know more than you do about what will work. It's okay for the vision to be about a step you are taking rather than the next hundred years. The important thing is that whatever you say, you are prepared to deliver on it as a solemn commitment. People quit believing when promises are not kept and nothing happens as a result.

The leaders of one organization took four tries before creating a vision that met all the criteria outlined in this section. In the past they had framed visions that were quickly penned but that no one around the table truly believed in. It would be nice if these earlier visions had come to pass, but no one really expected them to. Then a new leader insisted that the vision meet the tests outlined here. At first the team did what they had always done; but when the new leader tested their commitment, they admitted that it was not 100 percent. So, they tried again, and again. They admitted they had failed in the past because they had not lived up to their own stated commitments. It was not until they talked about their behavior and what was getting in the way of their full commitment that they could approach the task with a different intent. Even then they fell short when they tried the third time. More discussion, deeper dialogue, and breakthroughs in the level of honest give-and-take around the table were required before they could say that they were completely committed to making the new vision work—and it did.

Because the senior team's commitment to the vision is so essential, this is not a task that the senior team can delegate to others. Input from others can be sought and incorporated, but the final statement has to be the team's own.

People always ask about the wording of visions: Should they be one to three words long so that people can remember them, or is it better to have something that is a page or two with all the detail? Should it include specific targets, or is that a plan rather than a vision? Should it be inspirational or practical?

The vision serves a purpose in helping manage complex, continuous change. It provides guidance to the other processes we will discuss. It is more than inspirational. The last thing we need when facing complex, continuous change is for people to be fired up to take action but have no idea what that action might be or how their actions are aligned with those of others. Even if people can remember one to three words more easily than a whole page, having them commit the vision to memory serves no purpose if it doesn't help them make the right decisions. Visions cannot be so long that no one reads them, but they can't be so short that they are meaningless. They should do all the things discussed in this section, in a few paragraphs rather than just a few words. There can be a short title for the vision once it is written, but people in the organization should understand that the title refers to the vision as outlined in the longer document and is more than the words in the title alone. Yes, it's less easily communicated, but the goal is to achieve the vision, which will require that people understand enough about it to make good decisions. Such visions are harder to write than one-liners or documents with 50 pages of explanation. Just like managing complex, continuous change, it requires that you *think fewer*: focus on the messages that are really important, and do not allow the details to overwhelm the listener.

I love the old Toys"R"Us vision, for example, but it was too broad to provide much direction during complex, continuous change:

> Our vision is to put joy in kids' hearts and a smile on parents' faces.[5]

The new vision, "To be the World's Greatest Kids' Brand," may be a bit clearer but still doesn't say much about the *how*.

Amazon's vision is a little more specific. It places a focus on customers and says what the business model should enable:

> Our vision is to be Earth's most customer centric company; to build a place where people can come to find and discover anything they might want to buy online.[6]

When faced with too many choices, the vision should help people make the right ones. Even these visions could be clearer about the timeframe, specific goals, and approaches to be employed. Visions can have both long-term, enduring aspects that never change as well as shorter-term aspirations that point to next steps. Visions are not an action plan; they should be aspirational not operational. At the same time, they need to do more than make people feel good.

Think Fewer

The mindset that accompanies Discovery is *think fewer*. While the Discovering process calls for casting a wide net to detect weak signals that could affect your business model, rigor is required to focus on the few things to which you really need to pay attention. If the vision is too broad, it will fail in execution. Even a narrow agenda involves more work than most leaders imagine. Because change is complex and continuous, adopting an overwhelming agenda can actually hamper efforts to remain agile in the face of the unknown. Narrow the focus, and think fewer rather than more as you consider the actions that should be taken to keep the organization moving ahead. Make every change initiative count. Step away from the buffet of possibilities but don't just "stick to the knitting"; make an effort to change something that is important to better position the organization for what is to come.

4

Deciding: Think Scarcer

A S NOTED PREVIOUSLY, you can be good at anything you choose; you just can't be good at everything. There's a reason why the vast majority of Olympic athletes compete in only one sport; at world-class levels, it takes a dedicated focus to compete against the best of the best. Contrast this kind of single-minded focus with what you observe in your own life. How many things do you try to do at the same time? A short list for many of us would include excelling in our career; being a good parent/partner/friend/son or daughter; giving something back to others; keeping up with current events; finding time to refresh and renew ourselves—you get the idea. As noted by time and health coaches Jack Groppel and Bob Andelman in their book *The Corporate Athlete*, we don't live our lives the way Olympic athletes do.[1] We spread ourselves too thin and yet berate ourselves for not being successful in every-thing. We lack focus and discipline. We carry this tendency with us as we step into roles as organizational members or leaders. As you might imagine, it does not help us lead complex, continu-ous change. Yet we cannot seem to help ourselves. Groppel and Andelman advise that it is not the sheer amount of time you put into something you want to improve in your life that guarantees progress. It is the *quality* of that time. Pick a few things and do them with commitment and intensity rather than spread yourself thin. Seems like good advice for change leaders too.

In this respect Deciding involves more than compiling a list of things to be done. The former CEO of the consumer products company discussed in chapter 2 had a long list of change efforts under way, but those efforts had little effect. They were not prioritized or integrated, so investments in one often competed for time, attention, and resources with another—or actually worked at cross purposes. Proper Deciding requires *systems thinking*—the ability to see the whole rather than the parts, to understand where the least amount of effort expended will produce the greatest benefit, to seize opportunities to combine actions that produce impacts beyond their individual effects, and to monitor the system's capacity to digest all that is happening while maintaining critical performance commitments. This was the skill the new CEO possessed that the former CEO lacked. The former CEO believed that many independent change activities would produce progress. The new CEO understood that fewer, better integrated, and more powerful actions were what were really required. The former CEO dispersed his resources to fight a thousand fires as they popped up; the new CEO concentrated his resources on cutting a firebreak.

The objective of Deciding is to prioritize the efforts that could be undertaken to close the gap between the organization's current reality and desired future state, as set forth in the vision created during the Discovering process. Because complex, continuous change requires frequent changes in direction, Deciding is an ongoing activity that sometimes involves reversing decisions made a short time earlier. This should not be construed as needing to correct a mistake or seen as inefficient; in fact, being able to redirect activities is essential in a world characterized by complex, continuous relevant change.

Leading complex, continuous change involves diagnosing the extent of the gap between current reality and the desired state, examining options to close the gap, choosing which options to work with, and designing an approach to implementation that is both effective and realistic. The polarity to be managed during Deciding is to avoid doing too much at once while making at least as much change as the situation demands. Either too much or too little change leaves the organization in worse shape than it was in before. Finally, we should know that despite our best efforts, success will not be easy. Implementing change exposes flaws in the plans that are made during the Deciding process. Staying in touch with what actually happens as plans are implemented will often reveal the need to rethink the approach taken. This is the work of Discerning. In a world of complex, continuous change, an organization cannot afford to waste resources pursuing plans that are not working.

There are three key subcomponents of Deciding:

▶ Diagnosing: understanding the gap between the organization's current way of operating and its desired future state

▶ Focusing and prioritizing: developing options for closing the gap and prioritizing them

▶ Scoping and designing: making decisions about the extent of change, timing, and the approach that should be taken

Let's take the case of Chiquita at a time when the company was faced with an overload of opportunities and threats as it needed to decide how to compete in a market that had become both more complex and faster moving. President Robert Kistinger and head of HR Barry Morris, having conducted several rounds of strategic planning with the assistance of external consultants, decided it was time for the senior team to step away from the buffet and decide how to respond to the increasingly competitive and chaotic global marketplace for their product.

Although it may seem simple, producing fruit and getting it to market thousands of miles from where it is grown at exactly the right moment to sell, given a shelf-life of less than a week, is no easy feat. To aid in this, the company controlled all aspects of its supply chain: growing, shipping, and distribution. Just running the core business day to day and week to week was often hard enough without the twists and turns that weather, market prices, and labor issues added into the mix. But the company was facing even more complex, continuous change. The European Union was contemplating new legislation to favor its own producers. Customers were asking for special deals and mass-customization labeling. New regulations affecting operations were being passed. Each country in which fruit was grown was likely to renegotiate the requirements for conducting business there. Consumption in key markets was declining, which would necessitate moving into new, smaller markets. Other companies were interested in partnerships involving the brand. New product line extensions that would reduce the risk in the core fruit business needed consideration. Capital was required, and questions about the need to hold assets related to shipping and distribution had to be considered. The list went on and on. It was overwhelming.

The time had come to move from Discovering to Deciding. The company had already been through a few rounds of strategic planning with the best consultancies in the world. Still the decisions about what to do had to be made by Kistinger and his team. The choices were so important that Kistinger declared that making the decisions would be his team's primary focus until it was clear what the initial direction should be. Over a six-month period, Kistinger and his team put in the hard work necessary to review every plan and option. They assessed the pros and cons of each, which in some cases required that they collect additional information to understand the impact of a choice. They spoke to internal experts but also to external experts who knew the industry, as well as to potential partners, academics, and others who could help shed light on an option. In the end they loaded the most attractive opportunities into a matrix and evaluated each against the others, using key criteria the team had developed for that purpose. Following the intense examination of the options, cross-functional teams were assigned to implement the top priorities.

Not everything went as planned. Unforeseen forces affected the market and the organization, even with all the work that had been done. Some of the projects that were selected were not as successful as anticipated. Yet what really changed was that the organization was unstuck and moving forward. Rather than being paralyzed by complexity and alternatives, there was alignment on a reasonable set of priorities that would enable the organization to compete in new ways. Strategies on paper became strategies in action. The organization was no longer paralyzed by trying to do everything at once.

Diagnosing
Figuring Out What's Required

Diagnosis entails assessing the current capability of the organization to deliver against the vision. While it is tempting to build on strengths to close any gaps identified, it should be recognized that barriers to progress must also be addressed. The barriers will not disappear by doing more of the same better. Both driving change and removing barriers are required.

Kurt Lewin, the German social psychologist mentioned earlier, held that it is important to remove barriers before doubling efforts to create change.[2] His logic was that putting more pressure on the people to change when they can't because of the barriers only builds frustration. Once the barriers are removed, progress is relatively easy. He proposed a simple way of helping people think about this. On two sides of a piece of paper, he asked people to make a list of the forces that were driving and restraining change in the organization. He then asked people what could be done to augment or intensify the driving forces and, likewise, what could be done to remove or lessen the impact of restraining forces. In between these two lists is the goal that the organization is trying to achieve. As the restraining forces are removed and the driving forces are strengthened, the goal shifts toward completion. But if the restraining forces are not removed or the driving forces are not powerful enough, progress toward the goal is arrested.

This dynamic *force-field analysis* is a helpful tool for understanding why the actions that have been proposed to close a performance gap are not producing progress. It can also be useful in identifying specific actions that can be taken to reduce restraining forces or strengthen driving forces for change. While force-field analysis is good for understanding *why* the change is important (the driving forces) and *what's getting in the way* (restraining forces), it isn't good for understanding *what* needs to change about the organization to close the gap between current ways of operating and what is called for by the vision. For this, a more systemic approach to diagnosis is required. There is a catch, however: we often are very bad at understanding what's happening.

Dietrich Dörner, a German scientist, did groundbreaking work on how people approach problem solving under conditions of complexity.[3] We are faced with multiple complex, interrelated threats and opportunities at the same time, testing our ability to multitask by dividing our attention and effort across many fronts simultaneously. Unfortunately, it appears that our brains are not that different from those of our prehistoric ancestors; as a result, we are prone to making errors in our decisions about how to react. Using simulations to study thought patterns leading to good and bad decisions (which lead to either thriving healthy, communities or disaster scenarios in the computer simulation, where one decision is connected to others and has repercussions over time), Dörner found interesting differences between good and bad decision-makers (see figure 4.1).

As you review the characteristics of good and bad decision-makers, which better describes the world you live in? If it's "good," you have a leg up on leading complex, continuous change. If it's "bad," you've got some real work to do. Of interest, Dörner found no relationship between successful complex problem solving and intelligence; just being smarter does not make one better at managing complex, continuous change. It is not just that you

Good Decision-Makers	Bad Decision-Makers
Think complexly; many things need to be considered when solving a complex problem	Think simply; if the most important thing is addressed, the problem will be solved
Make many decisions and learn as they go	Make fewer decisions and remain committed to them no matter what happens
Test hypotheses by gathering data to prove or disprove them over time	Assume that the absence of immediate negative effects means everything will be okay
Ask more *why* questions (why does that happen?; look for connections among events)	Let their involvement in projects blind them to changes happening around them
Probe more deeply into what is really happening to better understand what is happening	Are cynical rather than inquisitive when things go badly
Figure out what's important to pay attention to and stay focused there; don't allow their focus to be easily distracted by things that are urgent but not important	Assume that their hypotheses don't need testing
Think in a more logical, structured manner (first, second, third); don't try to solve everything at once	Jump from one problem to another; lose track of the bigger picture; allow themselves to become easily distracted by others
Are persistent (don't give up at the first sign of difficulty) but are still open to ultimately having to change their whole idea about how the system works	Throw out what is working along with what isn't working
Learn from experience but also understand what is different about each new situation	Pay attention only to data that support their point of view; explain away contradictory reality

Figure 4.1 Dörner's Characteristics of Good and Bad Decision-Makers

have smarts; it's how you use them. If we have the proper mindset, we can uncover things around us that are new and important.

The purpose of diagnosis is to understand why there is a gap between what *is* and what we want. If our process of diagnosing is riddled with holes, the actions we take to close the gap will probably prove ineffective. In a world of complex, continuous change, we cannot afford to waste energy or resources on dead ends or wrong turns. Here are some aspects of diagnosing that we should keep in mind.

Understand what's going on   The goal of diagnosing is to understand what is really happening. If sales are down, what's behind it? If there's a gap between the level of engagement you have and what you need from employees, what will it take to close it? If you aren't getting enough innovation from your research-and-development expenditures, what's the rub? We have all heard stories about organizations that have tried to fix problems without understanding what's really going on. The point of doing a diagnosis is to figure out what exactly is causing the gap between the organization's current and desired performance so that effective actions can be taken.

Most things are connected   Whether you are concerned about solving a problem or taking advantage of opportunities, closing the gap around a complex issue usually requires multiple actions. If sales are down, is it the salespeople? The products? The competition? Are customers experiencing a drop-off in *their* sales, which is now affecting yours? Brainstorming multiple causes for problems will help you ask a lot of questions, which is what is needed to figure out what will be required to close the gap.

There are two sides to every story   Every organization is composed of people who use tools, knowledge, and work processes within an organizational structure to accomplish things. When you ask what's really going on, it's tempting to focus exclusively on either the human or nonhuman parts of the organization (such as structure, equipment, and processes). In one manufacturing organization, for example, leaders could not understand why quality defects suddenly spiked. They presumed that workers had become sloppy about quality and were poised to implement a retraining program. After further investigation, including discussions with the workers involved, it was discovered that the company had switched suppliers for some of the components being assembled. The new components were cheaper but also of lesser quality. It was not that workers had suddenly forgotten how to do their jobs; they simply couldn't maintain the same level of quality with poor raw material.

In reality, people and technology interact, and it is the combined influence of both that determines how things are going. One group of people using the same work processes will produce different outcomes than another because of the different social dynamics in the groups. Likewise, the same people who you thought could never do the job in the old structure may hit it out of the park following a reorganization. Before jumping to the conclusion that either people or systems are the problem, make certain you understand how the two sides of every organization affect one another.

It helps to know where to look   Using a diagnostic model or framework can be useful in directing your attention to things you should not overlook in your diagnosis. In Levinson, Molinari, and Sphon's *Organizational Diagnosis,* for example, there is a comprehensive outline of questions that should be asked to understand organizational dynamics.[4] Other popular frameworks are out there, including ones by Burke and Litwin, Weisbord, and Nadler and Tushman.[5] All of these point you in the right direction and provide critical questions to ask. Once you master one of these frameworks, you can use it again and again to understand what is driving change, what is restraining it, and where to intervene.

Fresh eyes   One of the great things about human beings is that they learn. We also have some faults, however, including believing that what we have learned in the past applies to every situation that seems similar from that point on. This is particularly the case with important indicators of organizational performance, such as sales levels or profit-and-loss statements. Because of the importance of these reports, and the time we have spent trying to understand what they tell us and how to improve results, as soon as we see a dip in performance we think we know what to do. If our usual solutions don't work, we may redouble our efforts before coming to the conclusion that we really *don't* know what is different this time. Or, we may employ expensive previous remedies when there are better ways to address the issue.

For this reason we should begin our diagnosis with the indicators we use regularly, but bring in fresh eyes to analyze what is happening. If we already know what we are looking for, we'll find it. It sometimes takes a fresh pair of eyes to help us look at the world in a whole new way.

You get out what you put in   Like so many things in life, your diagnosis will only be as good as the effort you expend. In the face of complex, continuous change, it is tempting to minimize the amount of effort put into diagnosis, but that would be a mistake. Frenetic activity that is poorly guided due to inadequate diagnosis is not what is needed. Careful diagnosis can narrow the scope of actions taken to address the gap between what is happening now and what should happen in the future.

If you have done diagnosing well, you should produce a list of actions you need to take to close gaps that need to been identified. The problems with lists is that they can go on forever, the amount of resources needed to complete the items is not always clear, and the amount of interdependence among the items on the list can be hard to spot. For these reasons, to avoid overwhelming the organization with change, one of the most important things you can do to lead complex, continuous change more effectively is to step away from the buffet of options available to you.

Focusing and Prioritizing
Stepping Away from the Buffet

Once the most important gaps are identified, a plan for addressing them can be developed. While many actions can be considered, focusing on the few and creating a realistic scope for change activities is a must.

A story is recorded by Scott Dinsmore about investor Warren Buffett's thinking about priorities on Scott's online blog, *Live Your Legend.* A shortened version of it goes like this: Buffett is having a conversation with someone to whom he is offering career and life advice. He asks the fellow to list the top 25 things that he wanted to do with the rest of his life that he had not already accomplished. Once the fellow did that, Buffett asked him to circle the top 5 from that list. This was hard, so when the fellow had finished, Buffett asked him to confirm that the top 5 were indeed the most important. They were. Buffett then asked him to think about his plans for accomplishing those top 5 things. After some more time, with more help from Buffett, the fellow had a pretty decent plan outlining how he would get started on each of the top 5 priorities. When this work was finished, Buffett asked the fellow what he planned to do about the other 20 priorities on his list. The fellow replied that they were still important to him and that he would work on them as time allowed. To the fellow's surprise, Buffett said sternly, "No. You've got it wrong.... Everything you didn't circle just became your 'avoid at all cost list.' No matter what, these things get no attention from you until you've succeeded with your top 5."[6]

Evidence suggests that more of us need to listen to Buffett's advice. In fall 2014 at the Center for Creative Leadership, we carried out a survey (specifically for this book) of an executive panel of more than 300 individuals to examine prioritization practices. Respondents represented both US and global organizations. The results were eye-opening. Prioritization was found to be highly valued but poorly practiced by many of the companies represented.[7]

Approximately 77 percent of the companies experienced more change than they did five years earlier, and 86 percent of those responding felt it was "very important" that their organizations respond to those changes. Only 9 percent said that their organizations were "very effective" in responding to change; this is reinforced by their estimation that only 52 percent of change projects were on track and ultimately that a similar percentage of projects actually achieved their intended outcomes. This number is a little higher than the figures cited in the preface with regard to the percentage of change efforts that achieve success;

but self-reports tend to be a little more optimistic than objective assessments. Still even these self-reported results tell us that we need to do much more to make change predictably successful.

Part of the reason for the difficulties in responding to change has to do with an inability to prioritize. There was a significant correlation ($r = 0.56$, $p \leq 0.01$ for you statistics types) between perceptions of effectiveness at responding to change and effectiveness at prioritization of change projects. In responding to change, 21 percent of those surveyed estimated that they had more than 20 change projects under way simultaneously; 11 percent had more than 50! What is a person supposed to pay attention to when there are 50 important change initiatives under way simultaneously? At the other end of the spectrum, 3 percent reported no change initiatives under way; that is not a recipe for success, either. In the middle, 13 percent reported 11 to 20 projects under way, and 55 percent said they had 1 to 10.

When confronted with multiple change opportunities, all of which are very important, 76 percent of those surveyed said it was "very important" to prioritize those change projects effectively. Yet only 10 percent said they were "very effective" at prioritization, while 44 percent said their process for prioritization was not effective. It is even more telling to listen to how those with ineffective processes described how prioritization decisions were made in their organizations. Here are a few representative quotes:

▶ "They aren't. Everything is equally important, and we will add before we've finished anything."

▶ "Major change projects are prioritized by our executive committee, but those seem to spawn other changes needed deeper in the organization in order to achieve the higher objective, but resources for those are not acknowledged."

▶ "Crises occur; the VPs hide it from the owners and blame it on the corporate staff. Once the staff member quits, they realize there's too much for one person to handle and bring someone else on, then repeat the process."

▶ "Sadly we are not good at it at all. The leadership thinks all of them are equally important. In fact, this year we have 17 presidential goals. Each goal has multiple facets."

▶ "We identify all the issues that need to be addressed and then try and attack them all.…When folks raise the idea of trying to prioritize the issues, everyone agrees but no one seems willing to take an item and postpone it."

▶ "Whoever screams the loudest."

Alarming? Yes, but not entirely surprising. Most of us hate to choose. We don't like giving up on projects that we think are important or that give us a chance to make a contribution for which there could be some recognition. It's like we're faced with a huge buffet of choices and simply can't stop heaping food on our plate. We need to learn to step away.

Some who have learned this lesson have adopted a top-down approach to prioritization. This can be effective at curbing overindulgence, but it does not necessarily guarantee that good choices are being made because those making the choices (usually the CEO or senior team) may lack important data about the impact of the tradeoffs or fail to understand the full impact of their decisions on the organization. Here is how some people described the problems with using a top-down process:

▶ "Top-level management and cascaded down, which sometimes is ineffective because conflicts aren't properly managed."

▶ "Often at top levels by a few people and not very well or at least not consistently communicated to mid- and lower levels."

The better processes described were collaborative, with input from multiple parties working through a prescribed series of steps that narrowed the funnel of actions from many to few. In most of these processes, the view shifts from local to organizationwide, using multilevel or cross-functional team discussions, which are sometimes aided by clear decision criteria. Here are some quotes from those who used more-collaborative processes to prioritize their change efforts:

▶ "We use a resource planning tool and constrain the resources available in a key organization. Business units get their "fair share" of resources and must prioritize their projects to meet their growth and change objectives. They can go to senior leaders to fund more, but it comes at the expense of another business unit, so the business case must be solid."

▶ "We have an enterprise program management team that works with our top executive team (C-suite) to establish companywide priorities."

▶ "Inclusive discussion of criteria by which priorities are to be decided; senior officers are then responsible for fairly and consistently implementing the criteria in determining priorities."

We need to experiment with better ways like these to prioritize or accept that we will be overwhelmed by the opportunities and crises that confront us. We must learn ways to step away from the buffet.

Scoping and Designing
Laying Down Tracks

Effective prioritization should simplify scoping and designing the plan for action. Still you have to think about what is new or added in the context of everything else that is going on. Leaders of complex, continuous change do not just keep adding straws to the camel's back until it breaks. They keep tabs of what is manageable and take things off the plate to make room for important new work if necessary. That was the brilliance of GE's Work-Out program: it cleared the decks of outdated and unnecessary work to make room for what was coming.

Scoping and designing clarifies the answers to broad questions:

- ▶ How big?
- ▶ How much?
- ▶ Where?
- ▶ When?
- ▶ How?
- ▶ Who?
- ▶ With whom?
- ▶ In what order?
- ▶ What are we going to stop doing?

There will still be details to work out during Doing. The scoping and designing should not be so specific as to leave little room for input from those who are closest to the front lines and whose lives will be the most affected. Leaving space for their engagement is essential in building commitment to execution. Yet progress will be hampered without a plan and a budget that outline what is expected to happen at a medium to high level. What we want to avoid is the situation in which everyone is headed in different directions, following their own ideas, with no appreciation for ever needing their efforts to align with others'. This would sound absurd if it didn't happen so often.

Once tracks are laid poorly, it is hard to achieve coordination, change directions, improve performance, and do other actions that are a part of the strategy. We push for change, but the tracks restrain us. That's why it is important to do scoping and designing, looking both forward and backward at the same time. We don't want each new opportunity to cause us to change direction unless it is absolutely necessary.

The bigger the projects and the more that has to happen at the same time, the more important coordination in scoping and designing becomes. Thus one requirement for good scoping and designing is bringing together those who are leading various changes for the purpose of working through where the interdependencies lie and when different parts of the organization will be asked to step up.

The other requirement for good scoping and designing is knowing how to translate actions to be taken into actual plans that work. This can be harder than it seems. It is one thing to *want* a transcontinental railroad and another thing to actually build it, just as it's one thing to wish for a new product success or a smooth enterprise IT system rollout and another thing to attain it. Complex change is by definition *complex*. Many moving parts need to be coordinated, and things that are *supposed* to happen *need* to happen for things to stay on schedule. In building a railroad, when unexpected obstacles like rivers or mountains or mudslides are encountered, things slow down and new plans must be made. Although the unanticipated obstacles are different, the same is true of new product development. If it were easy, everyone would be doing it well.

Of course, there is a point to good planning, which is to make you better prepared to change the plan. Good plans help you take less time and waste fewer resources, including your time and energy. These things can be used to cushion the disruptions when they come along, as they almost certainly will. By scoping properly, you can avoid biting off more than you can possibly chew, making success more likely. By designing the right approach to execution, you will avoid traps and pitfalls that would otherwise be encountered. The goal in scoping and designing is not to achieve perfection; it is to avoid as much imperfection as you are able. Here are some guidelines that you may find helpful in scoping and designing.

Big picture, small bites   As we scope we should keep the ultimate goal of change in mind but break down the journey into much smaller steps. Quick wins instill confidence and provide some indication that we are indeed on the right track. Chunking change into much larger steps that take longer and are more complicated is dangerous because we travel much farther down the tracks before we discover that our route won't take us to our destination. Big investments involve big risks, provide little short-term guidance, and crank up our susceptibility to ignore data that suggest our approach may not be working.

Out with the old   People cheer when we take things off their plate that have not been adding value. Few people enjoy doing work that is meaningless. If the future is important and continuous change is the norm, we should have a way of regularly reviewing what people are doing and getting rid of work that is no longer a priority. We should request that people ask themselves, *What's important now?* and come to us with suggestions about work that should be eliminated.

If the work to be eliminated is larger than one person has responsibility for, we should use a process like GE's Work-Out to focus attention on activities that need to be updated or cut. Let's end the insanity of asking people to undertake complex change when their plates are already full.

Selective engagement   Although I'm a big fan of engagement, it makes no sense to involve everyone in everything. Broad-brush programs that provide information sessions or training for everyone may make sense for some kinds of change but not for others. There are times when experts or fast-movers or those most affected need to huddle up to get things done quickly and cheaply. Disrupting the work of people who have no dog in the fight can lead to negative feelings rather than the commitment you seek. If people need to be involved, because they know something important or will be affected by the decisions you make, by all means include them.

It is usually beneficial to clarify the roles people are supposed to play in a project or across projects. One way to do this is to use *RACI* charting: names down one side of a matrix, the roles people are supposed to play down the other. The acronym stands for *responsible*—the person in charge (only one per project); *accountable*—people whose performance assessment will depend on the outcomes of the project and therefore are directly involved; *consult*—people who should be asked for their input or opinion either because they have vital information or their own work will be affected even though they are not involved in the project itself; and *inform*—people who need to be kept apprised of the project and its progress so they will be able to support it when necessary. Using this process, decide who really needs to be engaged and who just needs to be informed that something is going on. *Think scarcer.*

Open budgeting   In onetime change efforts, there is a seemingly overwhelming need to set an upper limit on the amount that will be spent on the project. The problem with this is that no one really knows in advance how much a project will cost. Budgets set this way sometimes run out before projects end; and in at least some cases, projects are forced into hibernation as a result.

In the case of complex, continuous change, our mindsets need to shift from yearlong fixed budget cycles to more continuous *open budgeting*. Opportunities should not be downsized to fit what is available in the current year's budget if the opportunities are important enough to cause us to question the very way we are doing things. Open budgeting allows part of the annual budget to remain open to reconsideration based on how the year unfolds. While some portion of the yearly budget must be protected to support capital investments and fixed expenses, another portion should remain open to reallocation as new priorities arise.

How large this portion of the budget is depends in part on the ratio of capital and fixed requirements to variable expenses. Some organizations are in better shape than others to allocate open budgets due to their financial condition. But another determinant of the percentage should be how rapidly the environment is changing and how important it is that the organization respond to those changes. Back to the earlier discussion concerning "out with the old," unless we are willing to stop spending money on things that are less important to our future, we cannot take advantage of new opportunities as they arise. These are hard choices, to be certain; but they are choices that determine how much change is possible in a given period of time.

There is a reality to budgets that is often at odds with our dreams about the future. In scoping we need to temper our optimism with some down-to-earth limitations. We do ourselves no favor by taking on more than we can afford. If we ignore financial limitations, we try to do too much only to fail. The good side of financial limitations is that they should cause us to choose more wisely what to change. Make every dollar count.

Feed the winners   Some people think that the place to start is where change is needed most: those horrible units that are dragging down the performance of the entire organization; those units that have always had terrible cultures, low engagement, and poor commitment; those units whose leaders need the most help to understand what they need to do differently.

These units do need to change, but they are poor places to begin for all the reasons that make them poor in the first place. Change in these units is difficult and costly. Often changes in leadership, work processes, or technical systems are required. Even then a negative culture can be slow to respond to change. Presuming that we can actually help these units, better-performing units and leaders will not look to them as examples they should emulate. Instead they want to distance themselves from the remedial actions that were required to effect change.

If you are looking for the best place to begin, choose units with good cultures and good leaders who are interested in change. Let winners lead the way because they can and because others will want to follow. It is easier to achieve success with winners, which makes progress faster. Winners are better able to recover if something goes wrong and still have the energy to try again to get it right. Once you learn what works by engaging winners, transfer the knowledge to units that need help.

Manage the heat   One of the problems associated with too much change in too short a time is that the overload hits some parts of the organization harder than others. Even with good prioritization reducing the overall number of changes the organization is responding to, there will be hot spots—teams, units, or departments in which people cannot do everything they are being asked to do. When these people are central to change, overall progress can become impeded.

The good news is that if we pay attention to the overload, there are many ways to address it. We can add temporary help, postpone some work, assign some work to others, figure out more-efficient ways to get the work done, or eliminate the work altogether (reduce our aspirations). We cannot do any of these things, however, if we are unaware of the overload.

How could we not be aware? We might not be aware if those experiencing the overload think that complaining about it would be fruitless or believe it's their duty to do the best they can to get everything done, even if it is impossible. We might also remain unaware if we respond to the overload situation in ways that we think are effective but don't really eliminate the overload, or we treat people who bring overload situations to our attention as the problem.

To avoid overloads, we need to be able to detect them and, when we find them, take actions to reduce them. We need to plan efforts more carefully and monitor work more closely on an ongoing basis. Maintaining a *heat map* is one way to do this. It is a simple matrix in which teams or units are listed on one side of the matrix and change projects are listed on the other. The cells of the matrix indicate when work on various projects is required of people on each team or unit. In more-sophisticated versions of the heat map, the impact of the projects on the team or unit can be indicated by a scale of some sort (1 = low impact; 2 = moderate impact; 3 = high impact; 4 = very high impact). But even simple checkmarks or color coding (green, yellow, red) will tell us a lot. To make the heat map even more helpful, we need to add the third dimension of time—*when* the impact will occur. Then we see more clearly when there is likely to be a

	Project W	Project X	Project Y	Project Z	Total Impact on Team
Team A	4	3	4	4	(15)
Team B	1	1	2	3	7
Team C	1	2	3	2	8
Team D	3	2	4	1	10
Total Impact of Project	9	8	13	10	

Key: 1 = low impact; 2 = moderate impact; 3 = high impact; 4 = very high impact

Figure 4.2 Example of a Project Heat Map Indicating that Team A May Become Overloaded by the Combination of Project Demands

perfect storm of critical projects hitting parts of the organization at a time when they are least able to do the work they require. See the example in figure 4.2.

The value of heat mapping for scoping should be obvious. If we plan change in ways that avoid overload, we are ahead of the game. If we plan to avoid overload and still experience it, we may need to examine our behavior to learn what we need to do differently in the future to avoid similar outcomes.

Think Scarcer

What the president of the food company and his team learned was that they could not pursue everything that they wished they could. They had to think scarcer. They needed to recognize the limits of their time, expertise, and resources. Deciding to do more than they could manage, even though many of the options were extremely attractive, would have left them paralyzed rather than moving forward aggressively. By using rigorous prioritization criteria following a careful assessment of alternatives, they were able to put things in motion that allowed them to begin experimenting and learning from new ways of operating. How many organizations try to do too much or fail to do anything at all in the face of multiple threats and opportunities? To lead complex, continuous change, you must practice thinking scarcer.

Doing: Think Faster

THE OBJECTIVE of Doing is to engage the organization in executing the change strategy. The key thought in this component of the work is *faster*. Complex, continuous change does not lend itself well to a ponderous, wait-and-see approach to execution. Instead the organization needs to move as quickly as possible to gain the benefits of current efforts and prepare itself for the next. The real way to get faster at change, however, is the opposite of what many believe. Delivering top-down dictates and charging ahead before you have taken time to figure out what you are doing or to get on the same page with others actually slows down change rather than speeds it up.

My colleague at CCL, John McGuire, talks about "slowing down to speed up," by which he means that a little engagement, planning, and coordination can eliminate serious execution problems later on.[1] In the context of Deciding, I mentioned the polarity to be managed between maintaining a reasonable amount of stability and changing enough to meet the demands of the situation. Going slowly so that you can prepare to go faster is another polarity to be managed. It is not either taking time to plan or moving ahead quickly; it's both. We know from early experiments in creating high-performance systems that engagement increases the speed of execution by 30 percent or more. We also know that authentic engagement takes time as people learn about change and wrestle with its implications. We recognize that as much as we would like people *not* to go through the ending and neutral zone stages described by William Bridges in *Managing Transitions* before they can change, there is no way around it.[2]

People need time to wrap their heads around what the change means and get their hearts into it. The last thing we need as leaders of complex, continuous change is to have our followers all over the map in terms of resistance, denial, loss, betrayal, confusion, or jumping forward before they know what they are supposed to do. In this state not only will the current approach to change fail but future efforts will be weakened considerably as people associate change with negative outcomes for themselves and the organization. There is only one way to execute complex, continuous change, and that is to do it correctly. Cutting corners always seems attractive, but in the end it does more harm than good. Like a skilled racecar driver, you go fast without crashing when you know what you're doing, practice to gain experience, and have good reflexes once you're in the race.

There are three key subcomponents of Doing:

▶ Communicating: helping people understand what is happening and why, and listening to their concerns

▶ Engaging: enabling meaningful involvement for people in decisions that affect them

▶ Piloting and implementing: using rapid prototyping whenever possible to speed the pace of change while avoiding becoming invested in strategies that don't work

Communicating

Helping People Understand and Listening to Their Concerns

People involved in implementing complex, continuous change are busy. They have a lot to do just to keep up with their current responsibilities. The call for change can fall on deaf ears, be perceived as a temporary distraction, or cause disruptions to current plans. The more complex and significant the change, the more time it will take for people to understand what is being asked of them and the greater the potential for disruption. That's why the hard work of Deciding is so important; distracting people or disrupting their efforts is not something you should do more often than the situation requires.

Most of us are bombarded by communication while at work and as a consequence have some difficulty deciding whether to pay attention to messages or ignore them. When we are really busy and concentrating on getting something done, we strive to block out as much as we can. It is against this backdrop that communication about complex, continuous change takes place. Getting people's attention and holding it long enough to have an effective exchange of information is a challenge to be sure—but one that must be tackled.

Having the CEO announce important changes is a solution that many organizations adopt, and it's a good one, as far as it goes. CEOs do command attention, and it is always helpful to hear directly from the CEO that he or she is behind the change that is taking place. Communication by the CEO is not sufficient, however. Meaning-making happens *after* the CEO's speech, as people ask questions, raise concerns, discuss plans with one another, and begin to take action. For these important communications, others need to be involved. The mistake that many organizations make is that middle-level leaders hear the message from the CEO at the same time their people do. When this happens, middle-level leaders are no better equipped to provide direction to their people than anyone else listening to the CEO's words. Because there was no formal plan for communication, what takes place next is often both ineffective and counterproductive. What does an effective approach to communication require?

Loud and clear   For the message to get through, it has to be loud and clear. Making the message loud and clear is a two-part challenge.

Loud means making certain that people notice the communication; they must stop, focus, listen, and stay tuned long enough to not simply hear the message but understand it. There is no one best way to communicate that is loud. The right approach will vary depending on the organization and the specific circumstances. We know that face-to-face communications are more likely to be heard than a memo. We also know that even with the help of technology, in large, global companies it is not possible to design simultaneous communications that feel like they are face-to-face. A person talking on a video screen is better than an e-mail message but still not as engaging as a real conversation. Think carefully about the methods that will compel people to take a time-out to listen to what is being said.

Clear means that the message is focused, succinct, and powerful. Do not pack too much into a single communication. If you communicate only infrequently, you may want to take the opportunity to update others on everything that is happening.

This is a mistake if action is the goal. Say what is most important to say and leave the rest to other efforts at communication.

Team effort   CEOs or leaders of other units may be the best originators of communication, but they cannot accomplish a robust, two-way dialogue across the entire organization by themselves. Effective change communication is a team effort; before the initial communication to the larger organization occurs, other leaders must understand what will be said as well as their own role in communicating. Organizations that communicate effectively have a process for engaging leaders in conversations before key messages go out to others. Middle-level leaders may have as many questions or concerns about change as their direct reports. If middle leaders are shocked by the communication, they may become what some have called the "clay layer" through which no communication passes either upward or downward, just like a layer of clay in soil blocks water from running through it. Instead of being effective conduits of information, they become powerful blockers and resisters.

In complex, continuous change, communication with middle-level leaders must be ongoing rather than sporadic. Because things are constantly changing, it would be easy for middle-level leaders to miss a shift in priorities or overall direction when it is called for. When miscommunication does occur, leaders at all levels need to be able to offer explanations so that people putting effort into what they were doing previously don't feel jerked around for no reason. The more informed we are, the better prepared we are to engage others and keep them engaged.

The challenges that accompany keeping leaders constantly up-to-date are not insignificant. Deciding what needs to be done in reaction to what is happening takes time. Once a decision is made, it is important to communicate the information as quickly as possible, which does not lend itself to a regular communication cycle. Because communication needs to happen quickly, there is not always time to polish the messages or test them for clarity. If the same process is used for communication or the same people do the communicating consistently, the process can easily become routine and the information ignored. After communicating, testing comprehension and making certain that people are prepared to act on the information they receive takes time.

It is little wonder that almost every organization struggles with communication as one of its greatest challenges. Even with social media, getting the word out and making certain everyone is aligned is difficult. Yet not doing so is bound to result in problems, such as slowing things down, causing people to work against one another, or failing to change successfully.

Several things can be done to help. First, recognize that change is a team effort and that failing to communicate successfully makes it impossible for your team to win. Second, invest in a communications person or department who knows what they are doing. If change is important, so are communications. Third, involve representatives of the recipients in planning the approach. They know what it's like to work in their world and what their peers are likely to understand and appreciate. Finally, check to see whether your team is aligned—often. If you do this, you will be amazed at how frequently they aren't and you'll wonder how you ever managed change in the past.

Top-down and bottom-up   We all understand that communication is supposed to be two-way. A good rule of thumb is to spend as much time listening as you do communicating. Yet how often do you attend a meeting where someone talks for an hour and leaves five minutes for questions? The real objective of most communications is to convey essential information—period. Our mistaken belief is that once the information, whether written or spoken, has been conveyed, it will be understood and acted on as we intend. *Wrong.*

Given the pace of complex, continuous change, there simply is not time for one-way communications that are ineffective and generate more questions than clarity. If the message is important, time must be built in so that people can understand and then act quickly rather than stumble around in the dark.

From the recipient's perspective, the assumption is that the person doing the communicating believes that he or she has been sufficiently clear. Although someone may end a meeting with "Are there any questions?" this often is a signal that the talk is over rather than a genuine invitation to engage in deep dialogue. To ask a question or prolong the conversation, the recipient believes, is not what the speaker wants. In fact, the speaker may interpret questions as either a sign of incompetence or resistance—and who needs that?

If you desire to communicate effectively, you will need to design processes into your communications that ensure that information is flowing in both directions. You won't end your meeting with "Are there any questions?" but instead request that people form into small groups and generate a list of questions or concerns that will need to be addressed if they are to do what you have asked them to do. If people are engaged, some of their questions will be difficult to answer in the moment. You will acknowledge this and have a process in mind for studying such issues and later providing clear guidance.

Furthermore you will realize that at the beginning of an activity, people don't know what they don't know. You will keep channels open for hearing back from them as the work advances, and you will expect to change things based on what you hear rather than push ahead blindly. There's a reason why the military invests so much in perfecting communications back to headquarters from the front lines. The front lines are where things happen, and what happens there is often different from what was anticipated. Why would complex, continuous change be any different?

Finally, you will build in time-outs every so often just to listen to what is on people's minds. Because organizations are social communities, they do all the things that social communities do, both good and bad. They get excited and energize one another, but they also spread rumors that are false and may raise concerns. They make heroes out of some people and villains out of others. They fill in the gaps in what they know with what they imagine, for better or worse. Taking a time-out allows you simply to listen and to then help people course-correct, especially when the course must constantly change.

Emotional hook   Communicating the facts is important, but urgency is the product of tapping into emotions. People want to understand the message; but they also want to know why the message is important. Powerful communications, like moving political speeches, tap into the heart as well as satisfy the need to know. To grab people emotionally, share a personal experience of an emotional struggle with change or tell the story of someone who has struggled with change and succeeded. I attended the annual leadership meeting of one company that used the blind adventurer, author, and activist Erik Weihenmayer to tell the story of his successful quest to climb Mount Everest, overcoming obstacle after obstacle, as a metaphor for the courage required to lead change. There wasn't a dry eye in the house, and people continued to refer to the metaphor for the next few years.

Good communication takes some effort, but it is only the first step in Doing. Real movement begins with engaging people in actions to effect change.

Engaging
Enabling Meaningful Involvement

Communicating is a prerequisite, not a substitute, for engagement. Effective two-way communication prepares people to take action, but acting is fundamentally different from exchanging information. People can be well informed and still do nothing. They can feel included because they are asked for their input but still believe that they should wait for someone else to make things happen. You know this from your own experience. When the time comes for you to act, you experience both a mental and physical reaction as your brain and body connect. The surge in adrenaline you feel when you realize, *Oh—they mean I have to do something*—focuses your concentration and prepares your muscles to move. How many times have you heard other leaders say, "I don't understand why people aren't doing X; I've told them how important it is." Telling people to do something is not the same as engaging them. If you would like to dance with a person, you don't say, "Let's dance" and then remain sitting; you stand up, reach out your hand, and lead the person to the dance floor. The same is true of engaging people in change. What is different is that often we need the entire organization to be engaged. That's a lot of hands to hold.

To convey information, it is relatively easy to send an e-mail blast out to employees or to arrange for meetings to be held in every department or workgroup. It's more challenging to prepare leaders to engage their direct reports. When the whole organization needs to become engaged in the Doing part of complex, continuous change, there are three basic options to get things started: representation, repeated processes, and large-scale interventions. Each of these needs to be followed by local actions by individuals, teams, departments, and cross-functional task forces.

Representation   The most common form of engagement occurs through representation. A project team is formed to oversee the effort. The project team, which is representative of the parties who must enact the changes, designs the engagement strategy to fit the size and scope of the involvement needed and then oversees the engagement process as it is carried out.

Representatives should consist of both credible formal leaders and trusted informal leaders. Understanding how the networks in your organization operate can give you an inside edge when leading change. The key roles to identify in your organization are the energizers, experts, connectors, and brokers. *Energizers* are people who lead informally through the positive energy they display and the impact their behavior has on those around them. *Experts* are people who know the territory that the change addresses; regardless of whether they are in formal leadership positions, experts need to be tapped for what they bring to conversation. *Connectors* are people who are natural communicators; they are the nodes in the information grapevine, and they will communicate without being asked. The more these people know, the more utility there is in their informal communication efforts. Finally, *brokers* are people who have connections across internal and external boundaries, bringing to light the interests of different groups so that they can be acknowledged and addressed. Without the key brokers in an organization, overall communications across boundaries can fall 30 percent or more.[3]

When you plan communications, it is clearly not enough to rely on the formal hierarchy. The informal social network is a powerful tool that can be harnessed to support change communications. If the informal network is ignored, it can also be the source of miscommunication and resistance. During complex, continuous change, the informal social network is an important secret weapon.

Repeated processes The best examples of repeated processes have taken place in the quality arena, where teams have been taught quality control methods and then asked to apply them to opportunities they identify. Although a large investment is required initially to instill repeated processes, once it is made, engaging people in continuous change becomes much easier.

In the late 1970s and early 1980s, Ford made a big investment in repeatable processes while General Motors allowed units to decide for themselves which approaches to change they would follow. Ford's "Quality is Job 1" program had a significant impact on product quality and consumer perceptions. GM tried things that were arguably more innovative, but in the end they did not have as much impact. At the time, one GM executive told me, "We have tried everything somewhere. The problem is we haven't tried one thing everywhere." Internal competition, political battles, separate union agreements, and a host of other issues led GM to a decentralized approach. If GM had been able to learn from its wider range of experimentation, perhaps it would have surpassed Ford's success; but issues with transferring learning from one location to another reduced the value of experimentation to the corporation as a whole.

Other examples of repeatable processes are General Electric's Work-Out program, Motorola's Six Sigma, and Nordstrom's training in customer service. The design of repeatable processes should match the strategy for the organization and the nature of changes that are needed to close the gap between the current and desired mode of operating. Complex, continuous change will require at a minimum that people know how to come together, identify the causes of problems, perceive opportunities for improvement, enact efforts to change, coordinate with others as required, measure outcomes, and repeat the process as required. Periodic or onetime changes do not warrant this level of process development, which is why groups are often caught off guard when changes are required. Improving the organization's capacity to change is a priority if the goal is to change continuously and effectively.

Large-scale interventions   Representative engagement takes time, and repeated processes are best for handling changes that are of a specific nature, such as quality problems. Sometimes engagement is needed rapidly on a change that is emergent and not likely to be repeated. In these situations one option for engaging the entire organization rapidly is to undertake large-scale interventions, which are designed to bring large numbers of people together to undertake carefully designed steps to move from ideating to action. With the assistance of technology to enable the capture of inputs and vote on decisions, well-designed large-scale interventions can galvanize action within a department, across units, or even in stakeholder groups.

One interesting application of large-scale interventions, for example, was the work done by AmericaSpeaks's Carolyn Lukensmeyer in the Listening to the City forum held in New York in July 2002 after the World Trade Center attacks. The purpose of the forum was to bring together more than 600 citizens and community leaders to plan the future of lower Manhattan. The event triggered several more like it, allowing thousands of people to become engaged in shaping the architecture, communities, and services that would ultimately be developed. Bringing diverse groups together to speak to one another directly enabled actions to be shaped more rapidly than if the normal course of events had played out, where each group advocated for its interests independently, over a long period of time, with little impact or cohesive purpose. The benefits of this kind of intervention for organizations faced with complex, continuous change are obvious. IBM's Jams undertaken by then-CEO Samuel Palmisano are an example of putting this method to use to shape a company's vision.

Many communities and organizations have used large-scale interventions to do future planning, solve problems, and redesign complex work processes. Although they do take planning and require facilitation, large-scale interventions are one option for getting large numbers of people engaged in change quickly.

Whether representation, repeated processes, large-scale interventions, or a combination of all three are used to support engagement, the goal is the same: to transfer the responsibility for taking action from the few to the many. Whatever process is used, at some point people need to feel that adrenaline surge that comes when they realize, *Oh—they mean* me!

Piloting and Implementing
Rapid Prototyping to Speed Execution

One of the best things to emerge from the creative work that IDEO and other firms have put into design thinking is the practice of *rapid prototyping*.[4] Before the discovery of this process, researchers everywhere tried to perfect their formulas or designs before releasing them for testing. As it often turns out, accomplishing the last 10 or 20 percent needed to "finish" the design of a product often takes as long and costs as much as the other 80 or 90 percent. Because of the time and costs involved, leaders often decided to narrow their focus early on to a few carefully selected opportunities, pouring everything into them in the hope that they had identified a winning idea to begin with. When these ideas failed, it was costly to go back and start over; so rather than change the way things were done, even more careful decisions were made upfront about where to invest. This process never worked well because the learning that was needed to make the right calls occurred long after the decisions were made.

Design thinkers turned this around with rapid prototyping. The concept is to test ideas at the earliest opportunity at the lowest possible cost. The products tested do not even need to be functional; they can be mock-ups of what the product would look like or what the product would do if it were developed. The feedback gained by testing cheap prototypes produces better data than concept testing without the prototypes. People can say that they would like to have a product with certain features at a specific price, but their opinions change once they have access to a facsimile of the real product. What was attractive as a drawing-board concept is not as attractive when the product is held in one's hand and "used." Alternatively, as they observe consumers interacting with prototypes, designers may hear ideas that they had not considered. This allows them to build in features that will help the product succeed once it is fully developed.

The benefits of rapid prototyping to complex, continuous change are easy to understand. So long as one is a little creative, almost any change can be prototyped before being rolled out on a large scale. This reduces the time to implementation because less time is spent in agreeing on what the perfect change would be and more time is spent learning about how different change options would work. Thinking about changing the reward system to better align with the new strategy? Have a team try it out for a month and give you feedback before asking everyone to accept the innovation. Want to impress customers with a new exchange policy? Try it out in a few stores before introducing it nationwide. Need to build a new factory? Have workers simulate what the workflow would be like in a mock-up in a garage or warehouse before breaking ground.

In complex, continuous change, there can be a lot going on at the same time. Getting everything to work together as intended is not easy. You might be experimenting with a new reward system at the same time you are building a new factory. Using rapid prototyping to better understand how the components of an interconnected system work together can prevent problems that would otherwise necessitate rethinking and postpone success.

Even once prototypical changes are adopted, implementing them in a large organization involves more adaptation to local circumstances. It makes no sense to force requirements on people to follow instructions that simply don't work or make sense where they live. Instead implementation should be viewed as another opportunity to do rapid prototyping to find local solutions that work.

The "find local solutions that work" part is important. Even with effective communication and abundant opportunities for engagement, people still begin change with doubt and experiences of loss. These feelings, as we know, can lead to resistance or change failures as people don't do the things they need to do to experiment with new ways of working, persist through the awkward and messy transition period, and eventually become comfortable with new ways of working. Because good changes can die out before their benefits are realized, it is important to encourage local adaptation but not to allow groups to forgo change when they encounter early implementation difficulties.

Until they are implemented, changes are no more than ideas. The problem with vision statements is that they too often remain on paper or are hung on the wall with no manifestation in reality. The changes required to realize the vision are bound to be significant if the vision is both inspiring and challenging. Few visions end with the phrase *and going forward, we hope that everything remains exactly the same.* In fact, visions call for the opposite: a brighter future, a greater impact, more innovation, better performance, more-satisfied customers, and so forth. Often during the visioning process, people are counseled to ignore the difficulties associated with making the vision real so that concerns about costs, timing, or practicality don't blind them to the possibilities. But now, during implementation, the time to pay up has come. Those who dare to dream are asked to put their money and time on the table to make the dream a reality.

The analogies we should keep in mind for implementation are things like Special Forces missions, surgical operations, and rocket launches. Before these things happen, there is a good deal of planning and preparation. People are trained for their roles and know what they are expected to do. No one says, "Let's just say 'go' and see what happens." Furthermore, everyone is totally committed to success even before implementation begins. No one says, "Well, once we get started, we'll decide whether or not we like it enough to keep going." The unexpected is anticipated. Alternative plans are discussed, but everyone knows that solutions to unanticipated problems will need to be invented as the problems arise. People rely on their expertise and one another to find a way to achieve success rather than give up at the first obstacle they encounter.

You may be thinking, *Isn't the need for careful planning and training before change antithetical to rapid prototyping?* Yes and no. There will always be the need to undertake changes that involve new learning for the organization. As we wade into the unknown, we face uncertainties that can best be addressed through rapid prototyping rather than assuming we already know the correct solution before we have tried it. At the same time, the effectiveness of the rapid-prototyping process is greatly improved when at least some of the people who are undertaking it are well trained in their domain.

I know that there is no way that I could undertake a Special Forces mission, conduct a surgical operation, or launch a rocket on my own. I would need the help of experts who know these domains. On the other hand, I could contribute something to the discussion of the experts by facilitating their conversation. I could observe who is speaking and who isn't, whether ideas are being challenged, if participants seem to be recycling the conversation to solutions that have already been explored, whether they are paying attention to data that have been collected, and so forth. Experts, on their own, can fall into closed-loop thinking: *I'm the expert, so when someone questions my decision, rather than under-stand their concerns I simply remind them that I'm the expert.* The Bay of Pigs invasion during John Kennedy's presidency and the decision to launch the space shuttle *Columbia* are classic illustrations of this. Experts need to contribute, but they should not be the only decision-makers.

Developing the expertise needed to address organizational challenges requires an investment in talent and organizational capabilities. Formulating and implementing complex, continuous change requires these investments to prepare the organization for what it aspires to do. If you plan to launch a rocket, you will need some rocket scientists. Yet how often do we see organizations try to do the equivalent of launching rockets with people who have never done it before? In the race to keep up with the pace of complex, continuous change, we sometimes try to leap forward before we are truly prepared to do so. It's understandable, but it doesn't work. We fail and only then understand what was required to succeed. Here again is the paradox: faster implementation requires greater attention to training and preparation.

The secrets to successful implementation are committing to success, preparing well, doing high-quality rapid prototyping, and sticking with it.

Committing to success   Don't waste time on changes that, in the end, you will allow to fail. Save your resources for the things that you absolutely must do to respond to threats or achieve your strategy. People don't need distractions, and you don't want to earn a reputation for backing down when the going gets tough. Make certain that if you say change is needed, you mean it.

Preparing well   What does successful change require? A workable solution, the right talent and training, adequate resources, sufficient time, aligned systems, and a supportive context. Remove any of these elements and you throw up barriers to change that may be insurmountable. Because you will never have the time and money to do everything as well as it should be done, carefully manage the polarity between preparation and getting on with change. If you succeed at change more often than you fail, you are probably doing a good job of preparation. It just feels right to provide training before expecting people to change, for example. Good. Keep it up.

Doing high-quality rapid prototyping   Invest in good people and good processes as you prototype change solutions. The higher the quality of your approach, the faster the work is completed and the more often you will find a workable solution. If you are already doing this, keep it up and see if you can do it even better.

Sticking with it   Complex change involves setbacks. People become concerned or discouraged. Alignment is elusive. Yet none of these truths can be accepted as excuses for not making progress. Leaders of continuous change expect difficulties but demand perseverance.

Think Faster

Rapid prototyping helps us learn quickly and cheaply rather than betting everything on a single strategy and trying to make it work regardless of what we encounter. Thinking faster is important during execution. We cannot afford to get bogged down. When most leaders look back at change initiatives and answer the question, "What would you do differently the next time?" they answer, "Move faster."

If we see the need to move faster, why don't we? One simple answer is that we don't slow down to speed up. We don't do sufficient planning and preparation to align people, provide training, and make certain we have everything we need to move ahead with real speed.

Another reason is that we try to take on too much at once, and other initiatives get in the way. That's a Deciding problem.

And there's the issue of not knowing how to prototype a change before we commit to it. Backing away from a big change that isn't going well is hard for most of us to do. We try everything to make it work instead of realizing that there may be issues with our approach that we had not anticipated.

Having communicated, engaged people, and implemented change, it's time to take stock of progress. Understanding what happened and why is like solving a good mystery: once we do, we can apply what we've learned to get better. This is the work of Discerning.

Discerning: Think Smarter

THE OBJECTIVE of Discerning is to learn from experience to improve the organization's capacity to change over time. Learning may not be as important in onetime change efforts, but it is crucial in continuous change. Without learning, costly mistakes are repeated, confusion persists, and motivation takes a nosedive. With learning, confidence grows—assurance that important changes can be handled simultaneously without overloading the system or taking an unnecessary toll on those involved.

The US Army is well known for undertaking after-action reviews in which those engaged in carrying out a mission pause afterward to understand what went well and what didn't and why.[1] During these reviews, efforts are made to eliminate the effects that rank would normally have on the frankness of conversations. Privates are asked to speak openly to generals, who need to hear what the privates saw and did in order to learn from them and improve how engagements are led in the future. There are four basic questions: *What did we expect to happen? What actually happened? Why did it happen?* and *What do we need to do differently going forward?* After-action reviews are one way to begin Discerning. For Discerning to be of maximum benefit, the learning needs to be put into action through making adjustments in our approach to change.

One way to supercharge Discerning, as the example of the army's after-action reviews reveals, is to tap into the collective intelligence of those involved in change. If there is ever a time to access information about what is happening in the eyes of those closest to the action, complex, continuous change is it. The faster this can be done, with the more accuracy, the better. This means cutting out the middleman. No long chains of command that hinder information flow directly from the bottom to the top. Like in the army, the generals need to be in the room to hear for themselves what the privates are saying.

If people have concerns about speaking up, Michael Beer's strategic fitness process can be employed to help people speak truth to power.[2] It involves getting a group of 10 or so employees to interview 10 of their peers, quickly summarize the information, and present it in a meeting, where the interviewers talk to one another about what they discovered while the leaders of the organization sit outside of the circle and listen to the conversation. Then the leaders move to the inner circle and repeat what they have heard so that the interviewers can listen in and add additional data or clarity if required. After that, the leaders exit, formulate a plan to respond to the input, and then test the plan with the interviewers to see if it would address the concerns they heard raised. This simple process cuts through the usual fears and allows the truth to emerge so that leaders don't have to operate in a vacuum.

The strategic fitness process was used by consultant Magnus Finnström of TruePoint in association with Cardo, a billion-euro Swedish firm with two main lines of business: industrial doors and wastewater treatment equipment.[3] The company sought assistance from TruePoint when it realized that it needed a single global transformation strategy and a culture to support it. Leaders wanted the organization to become more integrated and customer-focused and to feature a high-performance culture. Finnström introduced Cardo leaders to Beer's five levers required to create a high-performance, high-commitment work system: a collective learning process, enabling truth to speak to power, managing organizational performance strategically, managing an evolution in organization design, and developing human and social capital.

Having honest conversations between leaders and employees was essential to building commitment, learning, and taking action. That is where the strategic fitness process came in. Working with Cardo CEO Peter Aru and Per-Olof Nyquist, Cardo's director of organizational development, Finnström invented a leadership development process that combined learning for executives through application of the strategic fitness process to address key strategic opportunities. Following multiple rounds of the program, Cardo began to show dramatic improvement. The work that leaders undertook during the program had a huge financial impact that increased over time as the process was perfected. Even more importantly, according to Aru and Nyquist, the culture began to change in ways that would support the change strategy. Cardo witnessed increased involvement of people, more encouragement for driving change, greater application of the tools that were introduced to drive performance, increased collaboration across functions and borders, and improved teamwork.

Whether you apply the strategic fitness process or another framework, the point is to overcome the effects of the hierarchy to tap the collective intelligence of those close to the action.

Discerning is another opportunity to engage people in sense-making that matters.

There are three key subcomponents of Discerning:

- ▶ Aligning and integrating: achieving second-order change

- ▶ Assessing: learning from the present for the sake of increasing future change capacity

- ▶ Adjusting: changing the way we change

Aligning and Integrating
Achieving Second-Order Change

As first-order changes are being prototyped and implemented, information is already coming in about the intended and unintended effects of these changes on others. We also learn that existing policies, procedures, systems, structural arrangements, boundaries between groups, behaviors, and differences in cultures or beliefs are limiting the success of what we are able to accomplish. The interdependencies and interconnections among parts of complex systems are what *makes* them a system; an organization would not be an organization if every part simply did its own thing. To be an organization or a system, the parts need to work together to produce intended outcomes. The challenge is that they often don't, which at best leads to inefficiencies and at worst leads to internal competition, politics, and conflict.

Take the case of the CEO of an aerospace firm who found himself becoming increasingly frustrated with his direct reports as they failed to fulfill promised improvements in their units. Banging his fist on the table and turning red in the face, he shouted at them, "You sat around this very table three months ago and promised me that you would do these things! Now you're telling me that they haven't been done. I want to know why!" The team members' eyes were downcast, staring at the table. The silence became uncomfortable. Finally, one person found the courage to speak: "My team is doing everything it can to implement the changes we discussed, but we cannot finish making them unless we have the support of Ted's team, but Ted's team is busy doing the things they promised you they would do." Then Ted spoke up: "That's right. And we would have those things done if we had the support of Susan's team, but she tells me they are too busy trying to do the things you assigned them to do." It became apparent that each person around the table was running into the same problem. Each team was working on its list of changes and getting nowhere. The CEO had assigned the changes, thinking they were independent of one another when in fact all the changes were interdependent. Without adequate time spent understanding this and lacking a way to work out the priorities, each team was unable to complete its work. Better effort at Discerning could have revealed the problems sooner.

One of the interesting things that becoming a CEO often does is to change one's perspective. Most CEOs, having grown up within a function or business unit, spend their careers focused on the success of the operations entrusted to their care. It isn't until they become CEO that their vantage point changes and allows them to see clearly what may have been happening all along: that people who should be figuring out how to work together are instead either ignoring one another or competing for influence. Like the aerospace CEO, they wonder, *Why can't these people see the big picture?* and *How can I get them to be a more cohesive team?* Personal career ambitions are a part of the problem to be certain, but so are many other forces that act as barriers to collaboration, such as reward systems that emphasize individual success over organizational performance, and budgeting processes that force people to fight with one another to get the resources they need.

These and other issues at the top of an organization are mirrored at lower levels, as individuals struggle to integrate their efforts to serve the greater good. When trying to make positive changes, barriers put up by other people or systems act as a brake, slowing down or stopping forward progress altogether.

The mindset in Discerning is to *think smarter.* What this means in terms of alignment and integration is that we should anticipate that second-order changes will be required to enable first-order changes to proceed. Because systems are made up of interconnected parts, we know that changes we make in one aspect of the system *will* force changes to occur in other parts of the system. Too often we make changes as though systems are *not* interdependent; we believe that we can change the reward system or terms of service for customers or introduce new products without concerning ourselves about the second-order effects these things will have. Because we do not think ahead, we are surprised that the changes we seek run into barriers and are not implemented or have less impact than we imagined.

In complex, continuous change, second-order effects happen all the time. The need to align and integrate actions or face the debilitating consequences of not doing so is ever present. Because of the way systems work, second-order effects grow *exponentially* with the rate of change, not just in a linear fashion, which is why it is so important to decide carefully which changes are most important to make and to step away from the buffet of opportunities to improve.

Understanding the second-order effects of change is not always easy, and aligning systems can be difficult and expensive.

I believe that one of the reasons why two-thirds of our planned change efforts fail to produce the results we expect is because we rethink them after discovering the second-order issues they generate. When others push back, saying that change would be too disruptive or costly, we abandon efforts rather than push on. To allow this is, of course, to accept the status quo, which is something we cannot afford to do in the face of the need for complex, continuous change.

The way your organization is designed to operate right now is the result of many decisions that were made over time, often with insufficient attention to the impact each decision had on other aspects of how the organization does its work. The systems, policies, and procedures that are now in place are the sum total of many efforts to make things better. The problem is that now they act like a spiderweb to trap new ideas and hold them hostage. Breaking free of the web of forces that define the current "way things are done around here" takes a big effort—whether it's blowing things up and starting over or chipping away at change incrementally over a long period of time.

Your organization has a set point that keeps its performance close to the status quo. Without major change, you should expect small variations in performance around that set point rather than breakthroughs. Just as your weight won't change very much without diet and exercise, your organization cannot change until its ways of operating are realigned. Deciding where to start is the hardest part; after you begin, it's a matter of quickly or gradually bringing other parts of the organization into alignment, depending on the time you have available. The goal is to make certain that the parts of your organization are as aligned as they can be, given that things will continue to evolve and change.

Harvard professors Paul Lawrence and Jay Lorsch, in their 1967 classic *Organization and Environment,* studied firms in simple, slow-changing industries and complex, rapidly changing industries.[4] What they found was interesting. Firms that were in faster-moving industries were more complex internally, with more departments staffed by specialists. It seems that the added complexity called for additional expertise; generalist managers found it difficult to keep up with all the areas that they needed to understand in depth to guide their organization through the multiple, rapid changes required. That makes sense and by itself would not have made news. What they also found was more surprising: the more-successful firms in faster industries also did much more to connect their specialists, so as they became more differentiated internally, they also became more *integrated.* Having smart people is good, but not if they think independently and pull the organization in different directions. The bottom line is that as things get more complex, alignment becomes even more important to success.

How might you achieve better alignment and integration in your organization? Here are some lessons learned.

Alternate between getting on the balcony and mingling on the dance floor   You need to gather data about how the organization is operating after changes have been made. You should try to understand where things are going well and where they are not and why. To do this you need to be close to the action, listening to the voices of the people trying to make things happen. At the same time, if you stay in the middle of the fray you will find it confusing and difficult to provide meaningful direction. Leaders who listen to one direct report after another come into their office to complain and then give each of them what they ask for, even if it contradicts what others want, are not helping the situation.

As Ronald Heifetz noted, to see the big picture, stay attuned to the strategic goals you want to achieve, and focus efforts on a few meaningful priorities, you need to rise above it all. Discerning the impact that changes you have made are having on how the system operates is the first step in deciding what needs to happen next. The best way to do this is to alternate between diving down into the details and then pulling up and away to reflect on what you are learning. If you are always up in the clouds, you will know too little about what is really happening; and if you stay down in the weeds, you won't be able to see the patterns behind the challenges you encounter.

Focus on the greater good   In most situations there is a greater good to be accomplished. Often disconnects and conflicts that occur during change are the result of people's focusing too narrowly on their local interests rather than on what is best for the organization overall. While everyone would like their concerns to be addressed, the truth is that sometimes their concerns may not be important in the larger scheme of things. To align processes or priorities, something has to change. One party's political power should not determine who must give in and who can stay the same. Rather, the logic of how the overall organization is intended to operate should take precedence. Because there are quite often multiple perspectives and explanations for why things are happening, those responsible for Discerning need to exercise informed judgment rather than simply accept the opinions of others, regardless of their position power. To do otherwise would result in the system's being designed to make some people comfortable and others uncomfortable rather than optimize its effectiveness.

Manage stability and instability   Continuous change creates instability. There are limits to the amount of instability people and systems can absorb without malfunctioning. In the process of Discerning whether there is too much or too little change occurring in the moment, we can't be either insensitive to warnings about overload or too quick to slow the pace of change. When we realign systems, not all changes are equal in terms of their disruption. Some hit near the core, where changes disrupt everything around the core and often take time to work through. Others affect the periphery, where problems caused by the change have few ramifications on how the system as a whole operates. We need to Discern whether the pace and aim of change should remain constant or be revised based on what actually occurs as implementation takes place. These judgments can be made correctly only if the external demand for change is weighed carefully against the level of turmoil the organization is experiencing.

Resolve conflicts   Complex change inevitably creates conflicts among people who have different goals or worldviews. To succeed at leading complex, continuous change, we cannot allow conflicts to simmer. Unresolved conflicts stop action and leave parts of the system unaligned with one another in important ways. This is not the time to tolerate kindergarten misbehavior. Bring the conflicting parties together and force them to reach a resolution. Whatever they decide will probably be superior to a mediated solution or one imposed from above or outside. The people closest to the issues realize what's at stake; they are the best people to engage in figuring out how to resolve the conflict so that it does the most good and the least harm to the organization. Provide third-party help if necessary, but don't let the principals back out and appoint deputies to work things through. This is serious work, and the big players need to step up.

Forget perfection   It may be possible to achieve momentary perfection in aligning systems, processes, structure, and culture following a single change, but perfection in alignment is not possible when things are constantly changing. "Rough cuts" at alignment are better than trying to achieve watchlike precision among organizational parts. Instead of striving for perfection, do just enough in the moment and continue to enhance alignment as new opportunities arise. Second-order changes will lead to third-order changes, which will lead to fourth-order changes, and so on, for as long as the organization continues to experience change. Do not waste energy chasing your tail; do what is necessary and then shift attention to the next important priority.

Although perfect alignment is not the goal here, alignment becomes less problematic when systems and structures are designed for flexibility from the start. How to do that is the subject of other books. My *Creating Strategic Change* deals with this topic, as does Edward Lawler and Christopher Worley's *Built to Change*.[5] Both books make the point that we expend far too much energy in building organizations as if change will never happen, when evidence to the contrary is all around us. Perhaps organizational structures are a reflection of a deep-seated psychological need for knowing exactly where we stand in the world. Whatever the reason for over-structuring and change-proofing our organizations, we need to get over it.

A good example of this is in the area of job descriptions. In some organizations job descriptions provide precise details about the work to be performed. This is a good thing for pointing people in the right direction and eliminating potential overlaps of responsibilities. It is a bad thing, however, if the world is changing. Organizations like Google and W. L. Gore & Associates allow much greater latitude in how people define their contributions and in changing the ways they contribute over time. When every aspect of your organization is tightened down to the last bullet point, the process of achieving any kind of alignment as things constantly change becomes excruciatingly difficult.

The primary barrier to alignment and integration are turf battles between units. When these are allowed to persist, more energy may be put into keeping up walls than focusing on the greater good. Ending turf battles is not easy. Often the reason for them is built into the logic of the way the organization is designed. People in manufacturing (supply chain, these days) are supposed to concentrate on achieving maximum efficiency, while people in research and development (R&D) are dedicated to inventing new products that will by definition disrupt operations. That the two functions argue about the rate of new product introductions is a good thing. It would not do for manufacturing to block any new product introductions or for R&D to introduce changes weekly. On the other hand, it is a problem if the issues between R&D and manufacturing are never resolved, resulting in even less communication and alignment between the two.

In studying firms in the fast-moving computer industry that were more and less successful at new product introduction, Shona Brown and Kathleen Eisenhardt discovered that the more successful firms did a number of things to end unproductive turf battles.[6] The level of communication among internal units was higher; semipermanent forums were used to ensure that issues were resolved quickly; more new product introductions were pilot-tested before being introduced, to see if they really were good ideas; and additional efforts were put into consulting with futurists and strategists to make certain that products were in line with future trends. All of this additional effort resulted in new product introductions that were on time and did not experience the turmoil associated with turf battles in less successful companies. The bottom line is not to accept unproductive turf battles just because they have always existed. The parties need to be guided to engage in productive discussions for the greater good.

Assessing
Learning to Increase Change Capacity

Success in leading complex, continuous change is not marked by achieving a onetime level of performance against goals because goals are always advancing as customers and competitors demand that the bar be raised. We should, however, track both the rate of performance improvement in key measures and the degree of organizational alignment over time. Just as a reminder, in Discovering we are assessing the external competitive environment to identify future opportunities. In Discerning we should be focused internally on progress being made toward the vision. Here are some guidelines for conducting productive assessments.

Assess against the right goals   If we are trying to get better at change, it makes sense to assess our progress against the right goals. As the vision changes, so should the measures used to assess progress. Yet many organizations routinely track measures that are easy to obtain but no longer meaningful. *Thinking smarter* about assessment means reviewing the measures that are in place, making certain that they convey useful information about the current situation, and eliminating the wasted effort associated with tracking measures that add little valuable guidance regarding progress toward the vision.

For example, as IBM shifted from a computer hardware manufacturer to a service/solutions provider, many things changed, including allowing IBM consultants to use other manufacturers' equipment in solutions for clients if that was the client's preference. Continuing to track IBM's hardware sales as the primary measure of company performance under the new rules would have been a mistake. Instead declines in hardware sales could be taken as a sign of progress toward the new vision, so long as they were combined with increases in services revenue.

Make measures predictive   Most measures used to assess performance are backward-looking rather than future-oriented. Looking at sales, profitability, attendance, turnover, or employee engagement can be useful for establishing year-over-year trends. Yet there is no guarantee that next year will fall in line with the trend. Nor are such measures good predictors of the results of efforts expended to move an organization toward its vision in the face of continuous change. Instead of focusing exclusively on historical measures, develop a few that portend the future. Examples? How much are you spending on new product development, training, or business development? How many customer visits have executives made? How many new strategic alliances were formed? How many people took new assignments for their development? How many people attended conferences to learn about future trends?

With some effort, predictive indexes can be created that track investments in change activities or progress toward the vision. Because we focus on what we measure, just having these in place and reviewing them on a regular basis will help. If rewards are somehow aligned with these predictive measures, so much the better. The design of effective reward systems is beyond the scope of this book, but for a good discussion of the topic, see Edward Lawler's *Pay and Organization Development.*[7]

Don't guess, test   One of the most fascinating things about social systems (organizations being a subset of these) is the stories that people tell themselves to explain what is going on around them. Why are sales down this quarter? *Our salesforce just isn't motivated.* Why are we losing business to the competition? *They are stealing business by undercutting our prices.* Why are our new product introductions always behind schedule? *Innovation is hard for everyone.*

When we accept these stories without questioning them, we blind ourselves to other explanations and opportunities to improve. Rather than accept poor performance or failures to adapt in the face of continuous change, formulate multiple guesses about what might be going on. Then try out experiments to test your guesses. Is motivation causing poor sales? Measure the motivation of salespeople and see if it correlates with sales results. Try different incentives to see if they make a difference. Listen to what the salesforce thinks would help and try it to see if they are right. Are competitors stealing business by undercutting prices? Try lowering prices for some customers you have lost to see if they return to you.

The objective of assessing is to see whether the changes you have implemented are bringing you closer to your vision.

Whether you see improvements or declines, it pays to understand what is really driving the outcomes. Instead of making up interesting stories, conduct experiments to find the truth. You may even discover that the same people who are telling you that your change efforts are a waste of time are the ones who are sabotaging them. Stranger things have happened.

Check alignment   One of the goals of Discerning is to make certain that second-order changes have occurred to better align structures, systems, and processes. If these changes have been successful, how would you know? Here are some questions to consider: Has customer satisfaction with quality, order fulfillment, or customer service increased? Do employees feel that you are responding better to their suggestions for work improvements? Is less time spent in cross-functional meetings on settling disagreements and more time spent on ways to achieve greater alignment? If you ask people in different units to tell you what the priorities are for change, do they give you the same answer?

   If you track these or similar measures over time, you can develop a *goodness-of-fit statistic*—not the one you learned about in your statistics course but a measure that allows you to tell if integration is getting better or worse over time. Remember, it is relatively easy to let people do their own thing; it's much more difficult to bring people into alignment and keep them there.

Things to avoid during the assessment phase are not paying attention to what is happening as you change and ignoring the facts that you discover (if you do). Both are powerful temptations. Most of us want to believe that if we are working very hard at something, it is succeeding. Some of us, on the other hand, are hoping no one notices when we are not succeeding. It may be that none of us likes being assessed, but in the end only rigorous assessment can tell us what is really going on. Isn't that what we need to know to lead complex, continuous change?

Adjusting
Changing the Way We Change

The purposes of assessment are to take corrective action and learn from what happens so that future change efforts proceed more smoothly. As we capture insights over time, we can use them to guide investments in building greater change capacity at the individual and organizational levels.

Chris Argyris and Donald Schon are well known for their work in the field of change concerning what they termed *reflective practice*.[8] By this they meant learning from experience and applying those insights to adapting the way change is handled. They discuss "single-loop" and "double-loop" learning. *Single-loop learning* is when we notice that something is not happening that should be happening and address the situation without asking why it happened in the first place. For example, we notice that employees are not wearing their safety glasses as required and we put up a sign that says, "Wear your safety glasses." *Double-loop learning* is when we investigate why employees either forget or choose not to wear their safety glasses so that we can take steps to change the way employees think about wearing safety glasses, which will then translate into the behavior we desire. Rather than put up a sign that is soon ignored, we find ways to motivate employees to want to wear their safety glasses without being told.

As we assess the outcomes of complex, continuous change efforts, we learn that there are many things that did not go as planned. Each occurrence of this presents an opportunity to better understand how the organization really works. Kurt Lewin, the aforementioned father of modern organizational change theory, said, "If you want to understand something, try to change it."[9] Trying to change behaviors, systems, structures, and processes tells us a great deal about what people are invested in and why. Not all resistance to change is simply foot dragging. Sometimes there are valid reasons for wanting things that are working well to be maintained in the face of change. Good assessment processes should help us understand what is going on so that when adjustments in our approach to change are needed, we can make them.

For example, we know from both research and personal experience that communications are rarely heard and acted on the first time they occur. It may take six or more attempts at communication for the message to get through. If we presume that a single announcement is sufficient and then do a good job of assessing its impact, we will soon learn that we need to adjust our communication protocol. And so it is with other aspects of improving our approach to change.

The payoffs from changing the way we change are like compound financial investments. Adjustments improve results in the short term, but they also establish a new base on which future adjustments are undertaken. If we undertake the adjustment process correctly, the result will be an upward spiral of change capability. The organization will become more "change-able" and will use this strength to pull further and further away from flat-footed competitors.

Much of what we will need to adjust will concern the fundamentals of thinking fewer, scarcer, faster, and smarter. At the beginning of understanding what adjustments need to be made and then making them, it will feel like your first visit to the gym after a long absence. The going is tough, but it gradually gets easier as you do the work.

I love the metaphor used by Professor Kathryn Phillips of the Columbia Business School in a talk on diversity she gave recently. She said that some leaders she has known say that they are proponents of leveraging diversity but that they haven't done the hard work that learning to leverage diversity requires. She said, "It's like they go to the gym but just stand there. They tell everyone that they went to the gym, but they aren't doing the hard work to make them stronger."[10]

Going to the gym to adjust what isn't working in complex, continuous change requires a real workout, not just standing around. Ignoring reality to continue on as we always have wastes time and money, destroys commitment, and produces fewer benefits than we could achieve with the same effort if our approach was better. What does "working out" look like when it comes to adjusting our approach to change?

Not settling   If you've gotten this far, you know that the targets you set out to accomplish were important. Settling for less is the enemy of learning and ultimately winning. Reflecting on the reasons why outcomes were less than expected will lead to insights that can be incorporated into another run at the goal. If we employ double-loop learning rather than single-loop learning, we may experience a breakthrough in our understanding of how to change the organization. If instead we give up and accept mediocrity, we learn nothing. When we don't lose 50 pounds on our first trip to the gym (after we mostly stand around), we write off exercise altogether. Doesn't work. Might as well accept being overweight forever.

To be sure, there are times when, as we attempt to change something, we discover it is much more difficult and costly than we ever imagined. Sometimes you can't know these things until you try. If, after careful review and discussion of the alternatives, you conclude that the return on investment is simply not worthwhile, you have still learned something important: you need to do a better job of goal setting and prioritizing the changes you pursue. You need to be more realistic about the time and costs involved and better prepared to make the big investment if it is really worth it. If the goals of the change are not that important, you probably violated the *think fewer* and *think scarcer* rules by going after the change in the first place. It is not wrong to back away from change for the right reasons, but don't settle just because the going gets tough.

Act fast   Armed with the information gathered from assessing, don't spend too much time perfecting your approach before moving ahead. What assessing tells you is that you need to make a change in your approach. You will know something about what is working and what isn't. What you won't know is the perfect fix for the problem. You will have some guesses about what needs to happen. Don't spend forever researching them before pulling the trigger. Move quickly to try out several approaches in parallel if you can; you will learn faster than when taking time to speculate on how something might work.

Regrouping   Once you decide what you need to do differently, take a brief pause to regroup. Applying what you have learned to improve the approach you are taking may necessitate retraining or redeploying people. It could involve renegotiating with key stakeholders. It may dictate additional resources or changing systems, policies, or procedures before starting again. Just as when the change was launched, people need to understand what the new direction is and have the opportunity to become realigned.

The shift from one approach to another can be smooth if a little time is taken to carefully prepare for the redirect. Although finding time is always an issue when facing complex, continuous change, shifting gears without pushing in the clutch will result in a grinding sound rather than a smooth transition.

The net effects of Discerning are twofold. First, we fix what's wrong with our current approach to change. Second, we learn something that we can apply to future change efforts. Rigorous Discerning is not a cost; it is an investment that repays itself many times over.

Think Smarter

We can all agree that thinking smarter is a good idea. Most of us, however, are thinking as smartly as we can. To think even smarter, we need to rely on a process that will ensure that we are learning from our own experiences and those of others around us. There may be nothing more challenging. Whether you employ the strategic-fitness process pioneered by TruePoint and used by Cardo, or some other method, you must be certain to eliminate the weight of hierarchy and the sanctity of role boundaries to allow everyone to contribute. If you operate within the existing power structures, you will learn very little that is new. If you can set aside these structures, even temporarily, you will be amazed at what you Discern.

The four actions of Discovering, Deciding, Doing, and Discerning occur simultaneously and perpetually. For most of us, developing the capabilities to engage in them successfully requires training and practice.

Chapter 7 provides a look at what you need to know.

Building Greater Change Capacity over Time

WITH NO END TO CHURN in sight, it makes sense to learn how to respond to change at the pace the world is demanding. We have covered the actions required; now let's address how to continue to grow the capabilities needed to lead complex, continuous change over time.

Futurist Bob Johansen, in his book *Leaders Make the Future*, asserts that leaders need not be passive victims of change.[1] Rather he maintains that leaders can shape the future if they know how. This would certainly be helpful in the context of constant churn. Johansen lists 10 capabilities leaders should possess:

▶ *The maker instinct*—being entrepreneurial and action oriented; taking advantage of opportunities to make things better

▶ *Clarity*—being absolutely clear about one's purpose

▶ *Dilemma flipping*—seeing the opportunities that rising above seemingly opposing and unresolvable differences presents

▶ *Immersive learning*—knowing your field very, very well and knowing a bit about everything else too

▶ *Bio-empathy*—having a genuine concern for the well-being of the planet

▶ *Constructive depolarization*—Knowing how to defuse conflicts and bring people together

▶ *Quiet transparency*—sharing information openly and willingly to build trust

▶ *Rapid prototyping*—experimenting to learn rather than overcommitting to untested courses of action

▶ *Smart-mob organizing*—taking advantage of the resources outside one's organization to get help with answers or with taking actions

▶ *Commons creating*—establishing forums that bring people with shared interests together so that they can stimulate one another to do more

Several of these capabilities overlap with ones we have discussed as being central to leading continuous change: clarifying one's vision and direction is essential in Discovering; rapid prototyping is a key action during the Doing part of change; and immersive learning is part of Discerning. Some parts of the maker instinct, constructive depolarization, quiet transparency, smart-mob organizing, and commons creating are also implied in the approach outlined here. These "futuristic" leadership skills will become more important as the world becomes more difficult to predict and control through traditional approaches to management. Planning, organizing and, controlling—the stuff of textbooks on management a half-century ago—seem futile if not counterproductive in keeping astride of complex, continuous change.

Where does one go to learn these capabilities? Perhaps to Apple, Google, Facebook, or IDEO; or maybe to the Design Thinking program at Stanford; or to Rita McGrath's, Kathleen Eisenhardt's, Ian McMillan's, or Paul Schoemaker's strategy classes. If these options are not available to you, you'll do what you have always done: learn through experience. The Center for Creative Leadership's research into how leaders learn has produced consistent results the world over. When faced with a learning challenge, 70 percent of what people learn is learned on the job; 20 percent is learned through mentors, coaches, and peers; and 10 percent is learned through classroom education.[2] This tells us is that if we want to become futuristic leaders of complex, continuous change, we have to throw ourselves into opportunities to do just that. It helps if we have instruction so that we are not learning the wrong lessons from our experience, and it also helps if there are others around us to provide guidance, support, and feedback. In the end though, we'll learn most of what we need to know from the school of hard knocks. But wait—is it just a matter of trial and error?

In his intriguing book *Outliers,* Malcolm Gladwell helps us understand that the best performers in their fields are not born that way—they practice their way into it.[3] In fact, he cites research that finds that 10,000 hours of practice seems to be the tipping point between someone who is very, very good at something and someone who is a true master. This presumes a lot of things: that one has an aptitude for the work, that one continues to learn and improve rather than repeat the same performance 10,000 times, and that one is fortunate to have the support and resources that enable engagement in such a focused activity as he or she progresses from amateur to expert.

Without proper coaching and mentoring (the "20 percent" in CCL's 70-20-10 model[4]), we can learn the wrong things and repeat them over and over again. A frequently used example is improving your golf swing. Spending endless hours on the practice range adds little improvement without professional instruction to correct mistakes. If you have a coach or mentor who understands how to lead complex, continuous change, take advantage of that support. If you don't, reading this book will give you some ideas to practice; it will not be all you need, but it may keep you from continually practicing the wrong thing.

If we assume that most of us put in more time than the standard 40-hour workweek, and for the sake of easy math put in 50 hours on average, 10,000 hours of practice will take us a little less than four years to accomplish if we never take a vacation. The actual math need not concern us. The point is that learning to lead complex, continuous change in a truly expert fashion will take some time. We should not expect that reading a book or taking part in a single complex change effort will be all that is required to become a complex, continuous change Eagle Scout. We have to dedicate ourselves to it.

Fortunately, there are endless opportunities to practice. Also good to remember is that we will improve along the way, so our organizations will benefit from our learning even if we have not yet become "outliers." It is still a great advantage, from the organization's point of view, that we are avoiding more mistakes over time rather than making the same mistakes repeatedly.

Of course, becoming better individual leaders of change only addresses our part of the bargain. We also have to help our organizations become better at continuous change. The best cyclist in the world cannot win the Tour de France on a child's tricycle. If our organization were a bicycle, it would be best for it to be lightweight and have multiple gears and good brakes. If your organization is not designed for speed and flexibility, you have some redesigning to do. Let's discuss what it takes for us, and then our organizations, to achieve real breakthroughs in leading complex, continuous change.

Achieving Personal Breakthroughs

American philosopher, psychologist, and educational reformer John Dewey once said, "As an individual passes from one situation to another, his world, his environment, expands or contracts. He does not find himself living in another world but in a different part or aspect of one and the same world. What he has learned in the way of knowledge and skill in one situation becomes an instrument of understanding and dealing effectively with the situations which follow. The process goes on as long as life and learning continue."[5]

How do we improve our personal skills at leading complex, continuous change? What does the literature on learning tell us about achieving personal breakthroughs in performance on challenging tasks?

One of the foremost authorities on adult learning is my colleague David Kolb. His theory, based on a thorough review of the literature and years of his own research into the topic, holds that for adults to learn, we need to go through a process that includes four steps: concrete experience, reflective observation, abstract conceptualization, and active experimentation (see figure 7.1).[6]

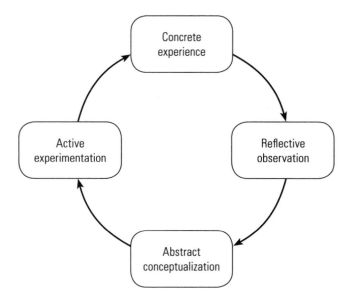

Figure 7.1 Kolb's Experiential Learning Cycle

As adults, we begin with a *concrete experience* that catches our attention and instigates the spark of curiosity that propels us to learn something new. The experience could be one of suffering a failure, achieving a success, or even just hearing about an idea that intrigued us. The concrete experience is the stimulus. In and of itself, it holds no value from the perspective of understanding why it occurred or even why it interests us. We need to dig more deeply to reap those insights.

People who are described as "experience junkies" are those who move from one stimulus to the next without regard for standing back from what they are doing to ask, *Why am I doing this?* They run on pure adrenaline and in fact are addicted to the experience itself, not to improving the way in which they understand the experience or might approach it differently to achieve the outcomes they desire. Managers who are in a constant firefighting mode when dealing with complex, continuous change are experience junkies. They thrive on putting out fires and solving problems. It doesn't matter to them which problems they solve or how they solve them; they just enjoy doing so over and over again. They define their value as being excellent problem solvers, without ever asking if there is a way to avoid the problems in the first place or to solve them in a way that improves the organization's long-term performance.

To understand what is causing problems in the first place or know whether the approach to solving them is good or bad requires stepping back to reflect on what is happening. This is *reflective observation* in Kolb's model. We talk about it as both Discovering and diagnosing here. To learn—or in this case to develop the capacity to lead complex, continuous change—we must first see clearly what is taking place. This requires observation, data collection, and an openness to inputs that may contradict what we believe to be correct or true. If we shield ourselves from the truth of what is really happening, we cannot learn; we see (and thus confirm) only what we want to see and already believe.

Once we have taken in valid information, we need to engage in sense-making—Kolb's *abstract conceptualization*. What is this information telling us about what is behind what just happened? What's causing this pattern? Why are sales dropping? Why are people leaving? Why was this product a success when the past 10 new products were failures? Sense-making is difficult because the information is often ambiguous and we are being asked to interpret it using a lens—a way of looking at things—that we have never used before. Sometimes we get help at this from experts who are familiar with the situation we are facing; at other times we have to make up our own interpretations. We may disagree about what is really going on. In such cases, we may have multiple alternative explanations for the same outcomes that we observed.

The only way to know whether our explanations are true or false is to test them. This is Kolb's *active experimentation,* which leads to a concrete experience, which sets the cycle in motion again. The more times we complete the cycle and the harder we work at doing each of the four steps well, the more we learn.

Kolb developed an instrument to measure our personal preferences for engaging in the four activities of learning, which he called the Learning Style Inventory.[7] If you are interested, you can take it in a matter of minutes to determine the part of the learning cycle you enjoy the most and therefore are likely to exaggerate at the cost of paying attention to the others. Because we cannot learn unless we complete the entire cycle, it's good to know if we have a tendency to fall in love with experience (experience junkies), spend too much time thinking rather than doing (planning, designing, analyzing), or try experiments with no hope of succeeding (taking random shots in the dark).

With regard to leading complex, continuous change, if I'm interested in learning so that I can increase my success, I need to ask myself the following questions:

- ▶ What is my current approach to leading complex, continuous change?

- ▶ How well is it working?

- ▶ What would account for the level of success I am achieving?

- ▶ Based on this, what should I do differently?

My *rate of progress* in learning how to lead complex, continuous change, like anything else I would like to learn, is determined by several factors. First, are there *consequences?* Does the learning matter? Are there ramifications if I lead change poorly or rewards if I improve? Second, how *committed* am I? Do I combine intention with attention to put time and energy into learning? Third, do I demonstrate *perseverance?* Do I remain committed in the face of setbacks? Fourth, am I surrounded and supported by my *social network?* Do they encourage me to learn rather than ridicule me for trying? Fifth, do I have the *opportunity* to learn? Am able to take advantage of learning opportunities that are moderately challenging? Am I given the authority and resources I need to act in these situations? Is it acceptable to learn from failure?

Breakthroughs in learning are usually the result of readiness coming together with opportunity. We find it difficult to perform at a higher level unless we have already learned the skills required to do so. Once we have prepared ourselves, we need the opportunity (sometimes multiple opportunities) to put our new skills to the test. If we achieve success, our learning is reinforced; we experience a breakthrough.

So, let's review. We are faced with the challenge of becoming better at leading complex, continuous change. We have recognized that our current way of responding to this kind of change is not working very well. We are overwhelmed with projects, and many of them are not producing results. We need a better way of doing things. There are consequences for failing to improve. We are motivated to learn.

To learn, we need support, opportunity, resources, and aptitude. Moreover we need to be willing to stick with learning through some setbacks and failures until we achieve a breakthrough in our ability. It can take some time before we see benefits that reinforce our decision to learn.

Creating the conditions for learning to lead complex, continuous change can be quite challenging. In the face of demands to respond to issues that are constantly emerging, we find it difficult to take time to step back, reflect, and learn. Yet, whether or not we are aware of it, we have a clear choice: to continue on as we always have or to invest in learning.

When few others have tried something new, we are reluctant to invest time and energy to explore it. It's better that we stay with what we know until some better way is well proven. Leaders in organizations who face slower-moving competitive environments may be able to ignore learning opportunities for a while longer. Those of you on the edge of chaos need to be learning now.

Achieving Organizational Breakthroughs

Improving our individual skills to lead change can be challenging. Helping our organizations benefit from what we have learned can be even tougher. What does it take to apply new ways of leading complex, continuous change to help our organizations navigate churn in the real world?

There's an old Indian saying that it is easier to help an elephant get up if it's already in the process of getting up rather than in the process of sitting down. If your organization is concerned about this issue, and has already designed some flexibility into how people approach their work, you'll be ahead of the curve.

Let's contrast a couple of examples. Some years ago colleagues and I decided to see if we could keep a manufacturing plant in Cleveland from closing, by engaging employees in transforming the operation. Executives of the corporation that owned the plant agreed that if we could improve productivity and reduce costs, they would reopen their decision to relocate production offshore.

The plant was very old, with outdated equipment and a traditional hierarchical culture. People were slotted into narrow jobs, most of which allowed little opportunity for creativity. Despite this the plant manager was a student of change and was interested in supporting our experiment.

We worked diligently for several weeks with the help of a number of employee task forces to come up with a prioritized list of changes to pursue. To our surprise, when it came time to implement the changes, we asked for volunteers to help with the implementation—and no one signed on! When we investigated further, we found that employees, having heard months earlier that the plant would close, had already made other plans for their futures. No one was excited about extending their time in a setting that they experienced as old, dirty, and unpleasant. They had little energy for trying to change an organization that had not engaged them in change before. They knew how difficult it would be to shift their culture, change the organization's approach to management, redefine their jobs, introduce new technology, and win the confidence of senior leadership. It was easier to simply exit and move on. The plant closed.

Contrast this example with Google, Facebook, or Silicon Valley startups. Their cultures are entrepreneurial, change is constant, roles are loosely defined, and people are dedicated to learning. Strategies shift as new ideas are explored or competitors make moves. Structures and processes are introduced but are designed to allow continuous innovation. People are expected to contribute their ideas. Leadership is top-down, bottom-up, and sideways, all at the same time.

Which of these examples (the plant in Cleveland or a Silicon Valley startup) would be more receptive to adopting new approaches to leading complex, continuous change? The answer is obvious. When rigid organizations face complex change challenges, they want to *control* how they respond. They want to divide their response into a series of independent projects, each with its own plans, schedules, and leaders. They want elaborate plans and regular progress metrics so that leaders can intervene when issues arise. They want to keep things under control, as if complex change can actually *be controlled.*

Entrepreneurial organizations *expect* change to happen and design for it. They leave room for people to react without central guidance, although they expect people to engage one another as they do so. Big decisions about major new projects, acquisitions, or company strategies are made centrally with a lot of input, but there is little or no micromanagement. People know what they bring to the table, but they don't know what work they will be doing in the future because priorities will change. Boundaries are permeable across units, teams, and levels in the organization. People are more concerned about the well-being and continued existence of the organization than accumulating power and influence.

When faced with change, these entrepreneurial companies do not try to formulate projects with precise budgets, deadlines, and metrics. They start working on things and see what happens. Projects shrink or grow with the promise they show and the excitement they generate. Priorities shift but not people's commitment to the ultimate success of the company. No one feels like he or she is working on a production line under tight constraints.

Everyone is free to comment and to try to contribute in the best way he or she knows how.

It is not that entrepreneurial organizations are better than more tightly structured companies. Each is designed to be fit for a purpose. Yet when it comes to being ready for complex, continuous change, the entrepreneurial organization has the clear advantage. If you are in a tightly structured company, is the situation hopeless? No. Michael Tushman and Charles O'Reilly have written extensively on the topic of *ambidextrous organizations,* by which they mean that organizations should develop the capability of operating in a tightly structured manner *when they need to* and in a looser fashion when that is called for.[8] Although learning to become ambidextrous isn't easy, there's no law against it. It just requires intention and effort. What keeps organizations from becoming more ambidextrous? Not laws of nature but rather leaders who say "we can't" or "we won't."

To achieve breakthroughs in organizational agility, leaders need to help their organizations learn by engaging in Discovering, Deciding, Doing, and Discerning. Just like individuals, organizations learn from practice, provided the learning is well directed and well supported.

Leaders need to support greater ambidexterity because no one else has permission to change the rules. At first the rules don't need to be changed permanently; they just have to be suspended for a period of time as people are invited to experiment with different approaches to continuous change. Once an organization gains greater insights into what works and what doesn't, more-permanent rule changes can be considered. Only then will true breakthroughs in responding to complex, continuous change occur.

The Multiplier Effect

When we consider the combined effects of leaders' learning about complex, continuous change and organizational readiness, a clear picture emerges. There are those organizations that will be good at change and, because they are good, engage in it, learn more, and improve over time. At the other extreme are organizations that are inflexible and led by people who are not highly capable of leading continuous change, who avoid change at all costs, learn little as a result, and fail to develop greater capability over time. It's the perfect storm. Consider the quadrants in figure 7.2.

It is only when leaders are skilled and their organization is flexible that the *multiplier effect* is experienced. For organizations that must change rapidly to remain competitive, this is a tremendous advantage. They change more easily to begin with;

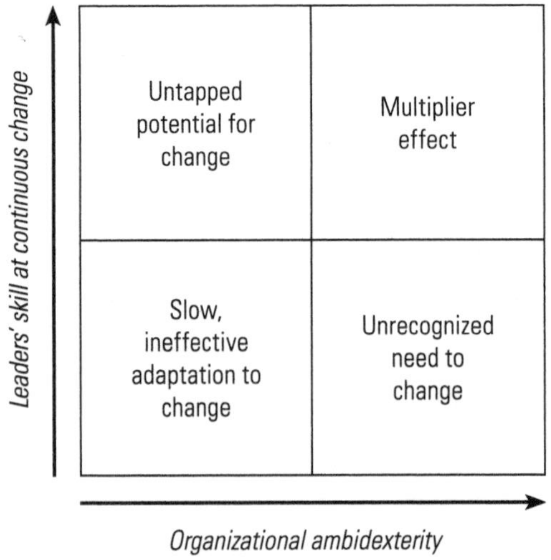

Figure 7.2 How Leaders' Skill at Continuous Change and Organizational Ambidexterity Affect Response to Change

and the more they change, the more they learn about changing. They get better at Discovering, Deciding, Doing, and Discerning. When faced with the need for even more change, they don't panic; they call on what they have learned to respond more effectively than their slower-footed competitors. Even if their response isn't perfect, they learn faster and implement new routines to do better the next time. Each time they take a step forward, they leave others farther behind.

It is clear that not all organizations are capable of achieving warp-speed change. It is easier to rewrite software code than to rip out and replace assembly lines. The standard to be concerned about is that for your industry. Are you faster than other Silicon Valley firms? Are you faster than other automobile manufacturers? You can also compare your current speed to your historical speed. Are you changing faster than before? Using fewer resources to do so? Prioritizing more effectively? Having more success? These are important things to track. Just as with exercising, if you don't keep track of what you are doing and the results you are achieving, you are less likely to make significant improvements over time.

The Role of the Adviser

In many of the cases reviewed in this book, an internal or external adviser played a crucial role in helping leaders understand the need to approach change differently. The advisers did not *lead* the change; that responsibility rested with the senior leader and his or her team. The advisers brought alternatives to the attention of leaders who were interested in achieving success in the face of complex, continuous change. They provided new tools and recommended the adoption of different mindsets. In some cases, they helped install new structures in the form of teams or standing committees who could assist with the process.

Having worked in the capacity of adviser over many years across organizations, cultures, and industries, I have had my share of successes and failures. Even though I'm well trained and experienced, there is no guarantee of success. Leading complex, continuous change isn't easy for any of us. As an adviser, I hope that I can be helpful but know that even when I am, the organization may be facing more change than it can possibly manage with the amount of time and resources available.

It helps to have a great partner in the senior leader. The CEO of the consumer products company described in chapter 2 was one of my best. He was a very sharp businessman who understood his industry and organization extremely well. His experience allowed him to correctly make intuitive judgments that less experienced leaders probably could not. He was ambitious, wanting to play a larger role in the parent corporation. He had accumulated a track record of success that gave him credibility internally and externally. He had an eye for talent and surrounded himself with the best while moving others out.

Despite his success and accomplishments, he remained open to change and individual coaching. He wanted to continue to improve his leadership as well as his organization and was willing to make the investments required to do so. He was not afraid to make tough decisions or take bold risks. From my perspective the most important thing he did was listen intently. He ultimately made the decisions, of course, sometimes not agreeing with me or going beyond what I offered, yet I never felt that he had made up his mind before we spoke. He was fully present and fully engaged.

As an adviser, I bring a few things. The first is an external perspective. I am not part of the history and do not have a deep investment in the status quo, so I'm not afraid to question things or propose different ways of working. Second, I understand change—deeply. I know what effective change requires and am able to point out when the current plan is likely to fall short and why. Third, I have skills in observation, data collection, and interpretation. I find ways to understand what is really happening by listening to a variety of voices, understanding patterns, paying attention to objective data, and listening to the things people really care about. I know I've succeeded when the clients I'm working with not only agree with the interpretation but adopt it as their own. Fourth, I build trust and credibility carefully so that I can influence people when it is important to do so. Change can sometimes feel like you are being asked to take a leap of faith—but you really need to take that leap.

At times I play the role of coach to an individual leader or team. There is as much work to do in private as in public. Before a leader or team stands in front of the organization to communicate, there is important work to be done in advance: ensuring alignment, agreeing on communications, and anticipating the unexpected are among the most popular topics. For all of my work as an adviser, I prepare like crazy but rarely follow a script. If I cannot demonstrate flexibility or openness to a different approach, I can't expect my clients to, either.

As I work with clients to undertake the four activities outlined in the model and cultivate the mindsets that support them, I don't tell them what to do, even though that is often what people initially expect of me. Instead I educate them about the thinking behind the activity or mindset and engage them in a discussion regarding the ways in which we could do things. I find that clients vary quite a bit in their preferences based on their belief systems or past experiences with change. I'm clear about what I think will *not* work, but I don't insist on my way of doing things. In truth, I don't have *a* way of doing things. I'm much more comfortable building ownership by involving clients in creating an approach that works for them.

Clients can and do learn to do this work for themselves. Once the processes and structures are in place and operating effectively, the key thing I bring is my external perspective. The rest they can do for themselves.

The Key Message and Guidelines for Action

Y OU HAVE BEEN on the roller coaster of complex, continuous change for a while. You may know what it feels like to live with continuous change with no way to deal with it effectively. If that is the case for you and your organization, it's not a comfortable ride. Now you know that there is a way to deal with it but that it is still challenging. It will force you to do some things that are new and may not be easy. You realize that things won't get better on their own. Change is not going away. If you want your organization to more effectively navigate churn, you need to take action.

What to do? *The key message here is that complex, continuous change is manageable but that it takes a level of rigor and focus that you may not have applied before.* The *first* thing to do is to pause. Stop, reflect, and do an honest assessment of how well your leaders are doing at coping with everything that is coming at them. Are they on top of it, with a clear, strategic, realistic plan of action? Or are they buried beneath it, adding more and more to the organization's change agenda without completing existing projects successfully?

The following are two hypothetical senior team conversations. The first is what it sounds like when things are out of control. The second is what you might hear once you have mastered navigating churn. Which one sounds more like the talk around your conference table?

Conversation 1 (out of control):

"How the hell are we going to get this new initiative started with everything else that's on our plate? I can tell you that my people are past the point of being burned out."

"Mine too. Still it doesn't seem like we have a choice. If we don't do this, we know what's going to happen. ACME is going to eat our lunch."

"I know that, but it's not like we aren't already busy. The things we are already working on are important, too. It's not like we can just pull the plug on something. We're way too far downstream to do that. If we don't keep going, we'll lose the investment we've already made in making those improvements; and there were good reasons for doing all that stuff, too. And by the way, we still have a business to run. When are we going to find time to do that?"

"I don't know. We'll just have to work smarter, I guess."

"Well, if you can tell me how to do that, I'm all ears."

"So, we're agreed we'll get this new initiative started this week, right?"

"I don't suppose we have a choice. I just don't know how we'll get it done."

"I'm sure we'll find a way. We always have."

Conversation 2 (under control):

"We've been doing our usual discovery work and have identified a threat we didn't see before that we absolutely should not ignore. We know we're busy, but we think we have to take this one seriously."

"Sounds like we should; but how important is it compared with the opportunities we're currently addressing?"

"We've been getting a handle on that by gathering data from internal and external sources. From our early reading, it could be right up there with some of our most important initiatives."

"Let's assign a team to work on it to see what might be involved in responding to it. Once we get more of a sense of what's needed, we can think about rebalancing our priorities. It could be that we have to postpone project X. I'd rather not, but if this turns out to be that important, we had better get on it."

"The team can tap people who have been through this kind of thing and can help us understand how much effort it took and what kind of solutions we might be looking at. Once we know that, we can decide whether we need to rebalance our project portfolio."

"We should put out a communication on this. We want people who can help us know what's going on. If we do need to change directions, it would be better if they had done some contingency planning."

"Right—no need to change course yet, but best to be prepared. If it turns out that this is as urgent as it appears, we'll need everybody's attention to work on a rapid prototype that we can use to test a potential solution. Remember that last time we took far too long thinking about what we should do before taking action."

"Good reminder. I'll start putting together a team spec sheet so that we can recruit the right people to help."

The first conversation reflects the heroic approach to leadership. Good soldiers keep trying their best in the face of impossible odds, knowing they can't succeed but never giving up. The second conversation is the result of efforts to step back, understand what is really important, and use a rigorous approach to focus energy on the most critical priorities. The exact words in each conversation are not as important as the tone. In the first conversation, the leaders feel like victims, unable to control what is happening around them. They literally do not know what to do. In the second, leaders are confident and poised for action. They have a process they trust to first understand and then deal with the situation.

As in other aspects of our lives, gaining control over what is happening takes dedicated effort. We may wish things would get better without having to work so hard, but we know the truth. We are not going to lose weight, learn a new language, or launch a successful product without dedicated effort. Therefore the first thing we have to do to get better at leading complex, continuous change is to *dedicate ourselves to the task*. In our personal lives, we can make that decision on our own. In organizations the senior leader and then the leadership team are the ones who must be willing to change the rules by which the game is played. No one else is allowed to do this. To be clear, here's what the senior leader and senior team must do.

Advice to the Senior Leader

The first thing the senior leader should do is take a step back for some introspection. If things are just fine, that's great. Consider yourself fortunate and do nothing for the time being. If you are concerned about the way your organization is responding to change, however, dig deeper. Enlist a fresh pair of eyes to help you see. It is extremely difficult to overcome our tendency to see the world as we are accustomed to seeing it. Conduct a rigorous, objective investigation into the state of change in the enterprise. What's working and what isn't? If necessary, bring in a trusted adviser who has the potential to scare you. This isn't the time for yes-men. Listen to what everyone has to say and decide whether further action is needed.

If you decide to proceed, insist that rigorous processes are developed for leading complex, continuous change. Hold people accountable for coming up to standard in Discovering, Deciding, Doing, and Discerning. Do not accept weak alternatives. The more rigorous the processes you install, the more progress you will make. Put in place people, processes, and structures that will make this happen, just as you found it necessary to do with quality, lean Six Sigma, improving the customer experience, and enhancing employee engagement. Know that you can do better, and don't stop until the processes are in place and working as they should. If they are, you should sense that the capacity of your organization to tackle complex, continuous change is steadily increasing.

At the same time, begin changing the mindset of members of your senior team. Discuss what it means to think fewer, scarcer, faster, and smarter. Help people understand the new reality: change will overwhelm us unless we take control of it. We will not win by trying to do everything and doing a lot of it poorly. We have to make certain we understand what's really going on. We have to make high-quality, well-informed, tough decisions about where to focus our energy, using a rigorous approach. We have to commit to what we decide to do and see it through. We have to execute well, making certain that we engage our people and others to help us. And we must learn from our actions so that we can do better over time. If we can't do these things, we will fail. Then, start checking your decisions to see if you are following these mindsets. Can you point to specific instances where you have thought fewer, scarcer, faster, or smarter?

You may find that the team that got you here is not the team that can take you there. It's not uncommon. Running a tight ship when things are not changing calls for a different skillset than leading during growth or change.[1] You cannot afford to surround yourself with people who are either complacent or heroic. You need objective, level-headed, highly capable, change-oriented people who are as dedicated as you are to doing things better. If you are reluctant to make changes in your team, convene a special task force to work on improving how the organization responds to change and lead it yourself. Eventually, you will need to get your team on board, but progress may be faster if you work with people who are excited about the challenge.

Finally, be prepared for the new approach to shake things up. If it doesn't, it's not worth the effort. Start thinking about lining up the internal and external support you will need to shift priorities, kill projects, sell off businesses, and realign governance structures.

The truth is, adopting a new approach to leading complex, continuous change will change the way *you* lead. If *you* don't make some changes, nothing else will change. As you think about stepping back, adopting more rigorous approaches to change, and taking on new mindsets, where will the biggest challenges be for you? You may need an executive coach to help you answer this question. Often others see us in ways that we cannot see ourselves. Do not let hubris or blind spots get in the way. If necessary, learn how you must lead differently. Leading complex, continuous change starts at the top. *You're it.*

Advice to Senior Teams

If you are on a senior team that is struggling with keeping up with the changes around you, first recognize that you are not alone. Having a sense that you're not on top of it all is not an indictment of your team or any of the individuals around the table. Nevertheless it may be time to do something about it.

The first thing to understand is that leading complex, continuous change is not something that any of you can do alone. It takes teamwork. If your team has problems working together, those issues are likely to be exacerbated by an inability to lead through change successfully. When important initiatives do not succeed, team members may begin to lose faith in their colleagues. Even worse, finger-pointing and behind-the-back politics may commence; these are definitely not helpful. So, if you are not already a strong team, you will need to become one.

How can you do that? Richard Beckhard, one of the founders of the field of organizational development, recommended a model for team building that has stood the test of time.[2] It is called the *GRPI model,* which stands for *goals, roles, processes,* and *interpersonal relations.* The big idea behind GRPI is that most of the problems teams experience are not because people can't get along; in fact, the reason they sometimes don't get along is because there is no alignment on goals, roles, or processes. If we agree on those things, there's a lot less left to fight about.

If your team is not as strong as you would like it to be, do a dedicated reset. Put some hard work into making certain each member of the team fully understands and supports the goals you are trying to achieve *as a team.* There are things that each of you needs to do individually, but this is about teamwork, so first focus on those things that you can achieve only if you work together and support one another; agree to make those goals the most important ones, even ahead of what you must do as an individual. Once you have authentic agreement (which isn't as easy to achieve as it sounds, so don't fly past this without really testing commitment to the shared goals), discuss the roles each person needs to play in achieving the team goals. Again, make certain that if people sign up for something, they really are committed to doing it. Third, make certain the *how* is clear to everyone. What are the processes you will develop and use? Then, and only then, set the ground rules in place that you want to follow as a team when it comes to how you treat one another. Once you have done all of this, commit to assessing on a regular basis how well you are living your commitments. You may need help with all of this because it's hard to lead team building from within. Beckhard is no longer with us, but you have access to internal or external resources who can assist if necessary.

You will need to engage in a similar process to agree how to lead complex, continuous change. You should agree on the goal. It helps to be specific. If you have 20 change initiatives under way, you might start with a goal of reducing the number of initiatives to 10. As you get better at using the processes of Discovering, Deciding, Doing, and Discerning, you can reset your goals, but in the beginning force yourselves to take action by putting a clear challenge out there.

Next, agree on your roles. Are all of you going to take part in changing how you lead change, or will some of you lead a team that does this on behalf of the others? Clarify each person's responsibility for the short and long term.

Then, put new processes in place for Discovering, Deciding, Doing, and Discerning. The more rigorous these processes are, the more progress you will make. Use the checklists in Appendix A to keep you on course.

Finally, provide one another with feedback on the efforts you are making as a team to achieve this important shared goal. Understand something that has been hard for many top team members to accept: *you will win only if your colleagues win.* As we compete for the top spot, we sometimes stand back and watch while others struggle. If you allow this, your team will fail to lead change. Failing at change won't help anyone's chances for future advancement.

Committing to making your team stronger and putting in place the rigorous processes required to lead continuous change takes real effort. You will need to make time on your agenda for this important work. At first it may take dedicated sessions or even offsite meetings. Later, as processes are put in place and become more routine, less time should be required. It would be nice if improving our capacity to lead change would come at no cost, but unfortunately that is not the case. Do know that if you can do this as a senior team, you will make a difference in the future of your organization and the life of every person in it.

Advice to All of Us

Organizations are feeling the effects of change, but so are we as leaders. We are faced with more complex, continuous choices than previous generations. We want to live the best lives we can, but like organizations we are frequently challenged and occasionally overwhelmed by the significance and velocity of the decisions in front of us. While I was visiting the good folks at Berrett-Koehler to discuss this book, several people pointed out that the advice given here would be appropriate for individuals as well as organizations.

What should you do? Step away from the buffet of life's choices for a moment to make certain that you can see the big picture. It is hard to make good choices when you're in the middle of the mess. If necessary, enlist others to scan your options. Distill a clearer vision for what you want. Decide what is most important to you by first diagnosing what's working and what's not, then prioritizing and finally designing your life. I have always liked the title of Mary Catherine Bateson's book *Composing a Life.*[3] It is a good read and, as the title suggests, it's about putting the power to shape our lives in our own hands. Once you know what you want to do, do it. Communicate your intentions to others whose support you need. Enlist them to help you; you cannot do this alone, even if you are ultimately in charge. Experiment boldly with new behaviors, but don't be afraid to change course if you aren't making progress. Be introspective, learn from what happens, and, if necessary, revise your plan based on your experiences. Over time learn how to do all of these things at once. Think fewer, scarcer, faster, and smarter. We get only this one chance.

If you are already doing most of these things, congratulate yourself. You are ahead of the game and far ahead of most of your contemporaries in navigating churn in the real world. If your to-do list is longer than you would like it to be, don't despair. We haven't been thinking about what it takes to lead complex, continuous change for that long. If you start now, and even make slow progress, you will still be near the front of the pack. Whether you will move quickly enough to win the race remains to be seen.

Riding the Comet can be scary or fun. You can choose not to ride, but the coaster is leaving the station.

Postscript

During the writing of this book, I came across the work of others who are chasing down answers to the question of how organizations can better manage complex, continuous change. The similarity of their conclusions to what you have read here is eerie, and I take it as a sign that we are converging on what may be some universal truths. I referenced the article by Donald Sull earlier.[4] Although Don's work is in strategy, his advice for closing the gap between strategy and execution is to make certain you have completed a cycle of four steps: *make sense, make choices, make things happen,* and *make revisions.* Different words but the same message. Christopher Worley and Susan Mohrman[5] address change management directly and also believe strongly that linear step-by-step models are becoming obsolete. Their recommended four actions are *awareness, design, tailor,* and *monitor.* They add in the center of their model *continuous learning* and *engagement.* So, there's more agreement than disagreement among us.

Before all of this, there was the famous *plan, do, act, control* sequence from quality control, which has some overlap with what we are talking about regarding change. So, despite some minor differences over terminology and emphasis, it seems that we all agree that there are four modes to managing complex change, each of which involves a slightly different character of work and set of skills to perform. It is a rarity when independent minds hit upon the same basic underlying structure when exploring new phenomena. It could be chance, but I prefer to believe that we're onto something that is real and important. Let's see where we go from here.

A Checklist for Assessing Where You Are

H ERE IS A SET of questions to help you think about what you might need to improve. Check the boxes to remind yourself where you may want to do some further work.

Discovering: Think Fewer

☐ **Right team**   Do we have the right seven- to nine-person team with the power, ability, perspectives, and credibility to guide us in looking at everything we are doing and everything that is happening to discover the few critical things we must attend to now?

☐ **Right process**   Are leaders committed to following the right process to discover what's really important?

☐ **Right data**   Have we analyzed data from a 360-degree perspective—internal, external, historical, and future?

☐ **Right conclusions**   Have we narrowed our focus to a few opportunities that will have the greatest impact? Have we stopped trying to do everything at once?

☐ **Vision**   Is our vision current, compelling, enticing, enabling, real, truthful, relevant, urgent, and personal?

Deciding: Think Scarcer

☐ **Diagnosing**   Do we really understand what's causing the gap between our current and desired future states?

☐ **List avoidance**   Are we doing more than making lists of things to do? Are we seeing the interconnections among things so that we know what few things drive everything else?

☐ **Sociotechnical**   Are we adopting a perspective that includes paying attention to what's good for both work and people?

☐ **Using a map**   Have we adopted a model or framework that helps us make better decisions about where to focus our energy?

☐ **Fresh eyes**   Have we invited people to think along with us who will challenge us to see things differently than we have always seen them?

☐ **Effort**   Have we put sufficient effort into deciding what to do, or have we blown past another opportunity to slow down in order to speed up?

☐ **Small bites**   Are we taking small, achievable steps while keeping the bigger goal in mind?

☐ **Cutting**   Are we throwing out old priorities to make room for the new?

☐ **Open budget**   Are we expecting budget allocations to change as we learn from experience where to focus and what change will require?

☐ **Winners**   Are we starting where success is likely rather than where it will be the hardest?

☐ **Hot spots**   Are we making certain the work does not overload certain teams or units?

Doing: Think Faster

☐ **Loud and clear**   Are people hearing our communications? Are they understanding them?

☐ **Team effort**   Are middle managers brought into the loop before communications go to their teams? Have we addressed their concerns? Are they prepared to help us communicate?

☐ **Top-down and bottom-up**   Are we spending as much time or more listening as we are telling? Are we really paying attention to feedback from the front lines? Are we engaging people authentically in ways that matter to them?

☐ **Emotional hook**   Have we made it clear why people should care? Is our message emotional and not just informative or good for the business?

☐ **Right people**   Have we tapped the informal network to involve the key people who will influence others to follow? Have we focused on the few rather than the many?

☐ **Repeated processes**   Have we invested in processes (like Six Sigma) that will allow us to use the same process over and over again to address new opportunities?

☐ **Large scale**   Have we leveraged the power of large-scale interventions to enhance commitment and alignment across the organization and with external stakeholders?

☐ **Commitment**   Are we truly committed to success? Have we made it clear that it's not okay to simply give up when difficulties are encountered?

☐ **Preparation**   Do we understand that putting time into careful preparation for change actually saves us time? Have we quit jumping directly into action before we know what we're doing?

☐ **Rapid prototyping**   Do we understand how to do rapid prototyping so that we learn quickly and cheaply what really works rather than overinvesting in approaches that will never succeed?

Discerning: Think Smarter

☐ **Varied views**   Are we alternating taking a helicopter view with keeping our ear to the ground?

☐ **Greater good**   Are we making the tough calls to do what is right, not what is easy or popular?

☐ **Modulating**   Do we recognize the importance of stability as well as the importance of change?

☐ **Resolution**　Do we work to resolve conflicts rather than leave them hanging and letting them interfere with progress?

☐ **Close enough**　Have we quit seeking perfect solutions in a world that is constantly changing? Are we willing to go ahead and experiment even if there is some risk involved?

☐ **Goals**　Have we adopted goals that are associated with achieving our vision rather than maintaining the status quo?

☐ **Measures**　Have we formulated predictive measures, not just metrics that tell us about what happened in the past?

☐ **Proof positive**　Have we tested our assumptions instead of making up stories about what is causing the outcomes we are observing?

☐ **Alignment**　Have we aligned our systems, structures, and processes to support new ways of working?

☐ **Speed**　Are we moving ahead quickly rather than needing to collect more data? Do we have ways to inform people and get them on board quickly without its taking months?

☐ **Regrouping**　When things do not go as planned, do we take time to reflect before employing a quick-patch solution? Do we at least pause to understand why things didn't go as planned?

☐ **Not settling**　When we do not meet our objectives after a good effort, do we try again rather than declare victory?

Leading Continuous Change Self-Assessment

A S MENTIONED in the preface of this book, you may be interested in this assessment that is intended to help you pinpoint your personal starting place in leading continuous change. The short 24-item survey will help you understand which of the four critical mindsets for leading change may need attention. The scoring sheet breaks down the four mindsets and helps you understand the perspectives you must adopt to be successful when there is more than one change occurring. As a companion to the organizational checklist in Appendix A, this tool will help you understand how ready you are to step up and lead continuous change.

Here is the link to the self-assessment:

www.bkconnection.com/continuouschange-sa

You may take the survey up to four times in a 12-month period. Bulk order discounts are also available for programs.

Notes

CHAPTER 1
Riding the Coaster

1. For discussions of the need for organizations to change to survive, see Clayton M. Christensen, *The Innovator's Dilemma: When New Technologies Cause Great Firms to Fail* (Boston: Harvard Business School Press, 1997); and Steven Krupp and Paul J. H. Schoemaker, *Winning the Long Game: How Strategic Leaders Shape the Future* (New York: PublicAffairs, 2014).

2. John P. Kotter, *Leading Change* (Boston: Harvard Business Review Press, 1996).

3. Kurt Lewin, "Action Research and Minority Problems," in *Resolving Social Conflicts,* ed. G. W. Lewin (New York: Harper & Row, 1946), 201–16.

4. Peter B. Vaill, *Managing as a Performing Art: New Ideas for a World of Chaotic Change* (San Francisco: Jossey Bass, 1989).

5. Marvin R. Weisbord, *Productive Workplaces: Dignity, Meaning, and Community in the 21st Century* (San Francisco: Jossey Bass, 1987).

6. Fred E. Emery and Eric L. Trist, *Towards a Social Ecology: Contextual Appreciation of the Future in the Present* (New York: Plenum Press, 1973). For a how-to guide to search conferences, see Marvin R. Weisbord and Sandra Janoff, *Future Search: An Action Guide to Finding Common Ground in Organizations and Communities* (San Francisco: Berrett-Koehler, 2000).

7. For an overview of large-group interventions, see Barbara Benedict Bunker and Billie T. Alban, *Large Group Interventions: Engaging the*

Whole System for Rapid Change (San Francisco: Jossey-Bass, 1996). For more on the world café, see Juanita Brown and David Isaacs, *The World Café Book: Shaping Our Futures through Conversations That Matter* (San Francisco: Berrett-Koehler, 2005). For additional information about the appreciative inquiry summit, see David L. Cooperrider and Diana Whitney, *Appreciative Inquiry: A Positive Revolution in Change* (San Francisco: Berrett-Koehler, 2005).

8. For an introduction to GE's Work-Out program, see David Ulrich, Steve Kerr, and Ron Ashkenas, *The GE Work-Out: How to Implement GE's Revolutionary Method for Busting Bureaucracy and Attacking Organizational Problems—Fast!* (New York: McGraw-Hill, 2002). For a description of P&G's approach to designing high-performance manufacturing systems, see David P. Hanna, *Designing Organizations for High Performance* (Englewood Cliffs, NJ: Prentice-Hall, 1988). The logic of Toyota's lean manufacturing system is laid out in James P. Womack, Daniel T. Jones, and Daniel Roos, *The Machine That Changed the World: The Story of Lean Production—Toyota's Secret Weapon in the Global Car Wars That Is Now Revolutionizing World Industry* (New York: Rawson Associates, 1990).

9. See, for example, Dane Stangler and Sam Arbesman, *What Does Fortune 500 Turnover Mean?* (Kansas City: Ewing Marion Kauffman Foundation, June 2012), http://www.kauffman.org/what-we-do/research/2012/06/what-does-fortune-500-turnover-mean.

10. Reports from McKinsey and KPMG citing these numbers include Matthias M. Bekier, Anna J. Bogardus, and Tim Oldham, "Why Mergers Fail," *The McKinsey Quarterly* 4 (2001): 3; and John Kelly, Colin Cook, and Don Spitzer, "Unlocking Shareholder Value: The Keys to Success," KPMG (1999), http://people.stern.nyu.edu/adamodar/pdfiles/eqnotes/KPMGM&A.pdf.

11. George S. Day and Paul J. H. Schoemaker, *Peripheral Vision: Detecting the Weak Signals That Will Make or Break Your Company* (Cambridge, MA: Harvard Business School Press, 2006).

12. Bekier, Bogardus, and Oldham, "Why Mergers Fail."

13. Bekier, Bogardus, and Oldham, "Why Mergers Fail"; and Kelly, Cook, and Spitzer, "Unlocking Shareholder Value."

14. Most of the background for this example came from Peter C. Wensberg, *Land's Polaroid: A Company and the Man Who Invented It* (New York: Houghton Mifflin, 1987).

15. Rita G. McGrath, "Business Models: A Discovery-Driven Approach," *Long Range Planning* 43, no. 2 (2010): 247–61.

16. Donald N. Sull, "Closing the Gap between Strategy and Execution," *MIT Sloan Management Review* 48, no. 4 (2007): 30–38; Shona L. Brown and Kathleen M. Eisenhardt, *Competing on the Edge: Strategy as Structured Chaos* (Boston: Harvard Business Review Press, 1998).

17. See Christensen, *The Innovator's Dilemma;* and Krupp and Schoemaker, *Winning the Long Game.*

18. William Pasmore, "Tipping the Balance: Overcoming Persistent Problems in Organizational Change," in *Research in Organizational Change and Development,* eds. Abraham B. Shani, Richard Woodman, and William Pasmore, 22 vols. (Bingley, UK: Emerald Group, 2011), vol. 19, 259–92.

19. For a discussion of change success rates, see Michael Beer and Nitin Nohria, "Cracking the Code of Change," *Harvard Business Review,* May 2000, 133–41, https://hbr.org/2000/05/cracking-the-code-of-change/ar/1; Michael Beer, Russell Eisenstat, and Burt Spector, "Why Change Programs Don't Produce Change," *Harvard Business Review,* November 1990, 2–12, https://hbr.org/1990/11/why-change-programs-dont-produce-change; and Scott Keller and Carolyn Aikens, "The Inconvenient Truth about Change Management: Why It Isn't Working and What to Do About It," McKinsey & Company report, 2008, http://www.csc.mnscu.edu/docs/ChangeManagement.pdf.

CHAPTER **2**

Leading Complex, Continuous Change

1. Jim Collins and Jerry I. Porras, *Built to Last: Successful Habits of Visionary Companies* (New York: HarperCollins, 1994).

2. Stephen R. Covey, *The 7 Habits of Highly Successful People* (New York: The Free Press, 1989).

CHAPTER **3**
Discovering: Think Fewer

1. Clayton M. Christensen, *The Innovator's Dilemma: When New Technologies Cause Great Firms to Fail* (Boston: Harvard Business School Press, 1997).

2. Ronald Heifetz, *Leadership without Easy Answers* (Boston: Belknap/ Harvard University Press, 1998).

3. Marvin R. Weisbord, *Productive Workplaces: Dignity, Meaning, and Community in the 21st Century* (San Francisco: Jossey Bass, 1987).

4. Gervase R. Bushe and Neelima Paranjpey, "Comparing the Generativity of Problem Solving and Appreciative Inquiry: A Field Experiment," *Journal of Applied Behavioral Science,* published electronically December 22, 2014, doi: 10.1177/0021886314562001.

5. Toys"R"Us, Inc. Corporate Vision and Values, accessed March 26, 2015, http://www.toysrusinc.com/about-us/vision-values.

6. "About Amazon.com," Facebook, accessed March 14, 2015, https: //www.facebook.com/Amazon/info?tab=page_info.

CHAPTER **4**
Deciding: Think Scarcer

1. Jack L. Groppel and Bob Andelman, *The Corporate Athlete: How to Achieve Maximal Performance in Business and Life* (New York: John Wiley & Sons, 2000).

2. Kurt Lewin, *Field Theory in Social Sciences: Selected Theoretical Papers,* ed. Dorwin Cartwright (New York: Harper & Row, 1951).

3. Dietrich Dörner, *The Logic of Failure: Recognizing and Avoiding Error in Complex Situations* (Cambridge, MA: Perseus Books, 1996).

4. Harry Levinson, Janice Molinari, and Andre G. Sphon, *Organizational Diagnosis* (Cambridge, MA: Harvard University Press, 1972).

5. A collection of different frameworks for diagnosing organizations is provided by the following works: W. Warner Burke and George H. Litwin, "A Causal Model of Organizational Performance and Change," *Journal of Management* 18, no. 3 (1992): 523–45, doi:

10.1177/014920639201800306; Marvin R. Weisbord, *Organiza-tional Diagnosis: A Workbook of Theory and Practice* (Reading, MA: Addison-Wesley, 1978); and David Nadler and Michael L. Tushman, "A Model for Diagnosing Organizational Behavior," *Organizational Dynamics* 9, no. 2 (1980): 35–51.

6. Scott Dinsmore, "Warren Buffett's 5-Step Process for Prioritizing True Success (and Why Most People Never Do It)," Live Your Legend (blog), February 1, 2011, http://liveyourlegend.net/warren-buffetts-5-step-process-for-prioritizing-true-success-and-why-most-people-never-do-it.

7. Center for Creative Leadership, "Experiences with Change" study, fall 2014.

CHAPTER 5
Doing: Think Faster

1. John B. McGuire and Gary Rhodes, *Transforming Your Leadership Culture* (San Francisco: Jossey Bass, 2009).

2. William Bridges, *Managing Transitions: Making the Most of Change* (Reading, MA: Addison Wesley, 1991).

3. Rob Cross, Peter Gray, Shirley Cunningham, Mark Showers, and Robert J. Thomas, "The Collaborative Organization: How to Make Employee Networks Really Work," *MIT Sloan Management Review* 52, no. 1 (2010): 83–90, http://www.robcross.org/Documents/Publications/SMR_Making_Employee_Networks_Work.pdf.

4. For an introduction to design thinking, see Tim Brown, *Change by Design: How Design Thinking Transforms Organizations and Inspires Innovation* (New York: HarperCollins, 2009).

CHAPTER 6
Discerning: Think Smarter

1. For an overview of the after-action review process, see Lloyd Baird, Phillip Holland, and Sandra Deacon, "Learning from Action: Imbedding More Learning into the Performance Fast Enough to Make a Difference," *Organizational Dynamics* 27, no. 4 (1999), 19–32.

2. Michael Beer and Russell Eisenstat, "How to Have an Honest Conversation about Your Business Strategy," *Harvard Business Review,* February 2004, 82–89. For a review of Beer's five levers that lead to high performance, see Michael Beer, *High Commitment High Performance: How to Build a Resilient Organization for Sustained Advantage* (San Francisco: Jossey Bass, 2009).

3. Michael Beer and Magnus Finnström, "Learning by Design: Developing an Engine for Transforming Your Company," *Leadership in Action* 29, no. 5 (2009): 3–7, doi: 10.1002/lia.1303.

4. Paul R. Lawrence and Jay W. Lorsch, *Organization and Environment: Managing Differentiation and Integration* (Cambridge, MA: Harvard University Press, 1967).

5. William A. Pasmore, *Creating Strategic Change: Designing the Flexible, High-Performing Organization* (New York: Wiley & Sons, 1994); Edward E. Lawler III and Christopher G. Worley, *Built to Change: How to Achieve Sustained Organizational Effectiveness* (San Francisco: Jossey Bass, 2006).

6. Shona Brown and Kathleen Eisenhardt, "The Art of Continuous Change: Linking Complexity Theory and Time-Based Evolution in Relentlessly Shifting Organizations," *Administrative Science Quarterly* 42, no. 1 (1997), 1–34.

7. Edward Lawler, *Pay and Organization Development* (Englewood Cliffs, NJ: Prentice-Hall, 1981).

8. Chris Argyris and Donald A. Schon, *Organizational Learning: A Theory of Action Perspective* (Reading, MA: Addison Wesley, 1978).

9. Kurt Lewin, *Field Theory in Social Science* (New York: Harper Torchbooks, 1951).

10. Katherine W. Phillips, lecture at Columbia University, Teachers College, September 16, 2014.

CHAPTER **7**

Building Greater Change Capacity over Time

1. Bob Johansen, *Leaders Make the Future: Ten New Leadership Skills for an Uncertain World* (San Francisco: Berrett-Koehler, 2012).

2. Morgan W. McCall Jr., Michael M. Lombardo, and Ann M. Morrison, *The Lessons of Experience: How Successful Executives Develop on the Job* (San Francisco: New Lexington Press, 1980).

3. Malcolm Gladwell, *Outliers: The Story of Success* (New York: Little, Brown, 2008).

4. Morgan W. McCall Jr., Michael M. Lombardo, and Ann M. Morrison, *The Lessons of Experience: How Successful Executives Develop on the Job* (Lexington, MA: Lexington Books, 1988). When leaders are asked how they learned what they know about leadership, they say that they learned 70 percent of the most important lessons on the job; 20 percent from peers, mentors, or coaches; and 10 percent from formal programs and education. While there has been some debate about the exact percentages since this original publication on the topic, the primacy of learning from experience remains undeniable.

5. John Dewey, *Experience and Education* (New York: Touchstone, 1938) 44.

6. David Kolb, *Experiential Learning: Experience as the Source of Learning and Development* (Upper Saddle River, NJ: Prentice-Hall, 1984).

7. David A. Kolb, *Kolb Learning Style Inventory: LSI Workbook* (Philadelphia: Hay Group, 2013).

8. Michael L. Tushman and Charles A. O'Reilly III, *Winning through Innovation: A Practical Guide to Leading Organizational Change and Renewal* (Cambridge, MA: Harvard University Press, 1997).

CHAPTER **8**

The Key Message and Guidelines for Action

1. For a discussion of the different skills of growth versus nongrowth leaders, see Katharina Herrmann, Asmus Komm, and Sven Smit, "Do You Have the Right Leaders for Your Growth Strategies?" *The McKinsey Quarterly,* July 2011, http://www.mckinsey.com /insights/leading_in_the_21st_century/do_you_have_the_right _leaders_for_your_growth_strategies?cid=other-eml-cls-mip -mck-oth-1501.

2. Richard Beckhard, "Optimizing Team-Building Efforts," *Journal of Contemporary Business* 1, no. 3 (1972): 23–32.

3. Mary Catherine Bateson, *Composing a Life* (Grove Press, 2001).

4. Donald N. Sull, "Closing the Gap between Strategy and Execution," *MIT Sloan Management Review* 48, no. 4 (2007): 30–38.

5. Christopher G. Worley and Susan A. Mohrman, "Is Change Management Obsolete?" *Organizational Dynamics* 43, no. 3 (2014): 214–24.

Acknowledgments

I WOULD LIKE TO THANK a number of people who contributed directly and indirectly to this work. Some are named and some are anonymous. My Center for Creative Leadership colleagues, Jennifer Martineau and John McGuire, were there from the start, offering ideas and encouragement throughout the journey. John Ryan, CCL's president, one of the best leaders I have ever had the privilege to serve, has been generous in allowing me time to work on this and went above and beyond to offer his own thoughts in the foreword, which I hope you read. Stephen Martin, Kelly Lombardino, and Peter Scisco have represented CCL's interests during interactions with Berrett-Koehler and added their own expertise in helping craft and market the book. Paula Morrow designed the survey and conducted the research with CCL's executive panel that helped us understand the current state of affairs with regard to the success rate at change efforts and how people are handling the challenge of prioritization. Portia Mount, CCL's senior vice president of marketing, has been generous with her organization's time and attention to this project.

At Berrett-Koehler the project started with the support of Jeevan Sivasubramaniam, who was extremely helpful in taking an overly complex book about continuous change and making it infinitely more accessible and useful. Credit for the title goes to him. Neal Maillet handled the editing responsibilities once the manuscript took shape, and BK's reviewers provided very constructive feedback, as did Steve Piersanti, Berrett-Koehler's publisher and president. He made certain the takeaways were clear so that people in similar positions would not wind up scratching their heads after finishing the final chapter. The rest of the Berrett-Koehler staff have been incredibly helpful. They do what they do in a very competent, organized, and engaging way. I feel safe in their hands.

At Teachers College my colleagues Warner Burke and Debra Noumair recruited me to help deliver an executive master's degree program on change leadership. Our conversations and the discussions I have had with students in that program have been another source of inspiration for the ideas here. Zach Kristensen, one of our students, volunteered to help with research for the book. Thanks, Zach.

My client partners, not all of whom I can mention by name, provided the opportunities that allowed me to learn from their efforts as well as test new ideas when there were risks involved. They are the ones whose careers rise or fall depending on how well they manage churn. They live in the real world, and I thank them for having confidence in me to join them there.

At home there's my wife, Mary. She has been there through it all. When you face complex, continuous change, it's good to have someone in your corner. Thanks for all you do to make this journey possible and worth taking. My daughters, Brenna and Kelsey, are only beginning their careers and think it's kind of cute that their dad writes books. I think they're kind of cute, too.

Index

About the Author

BILL PASMORE is senior vice president at the Center for Creative Leadership, with responsibility for the organization's global Organizational Leadership business. Bill also holds the position of professor of practice at Teachers College, Columbia University, in which he helps link scholarship in the field of organizational development and leadership to practice. He teaches in the college's doctoral and master's degree programs and conducts research in leadership and organizational change.

Bill's current work focuses on leading complex change, applying design thinking to organizational innovation, and using network analysis to accelerate change. He consults with CEOs, senior teams, and organizations on leading change, senior team effectiveness, collaborative strategic planning, organizational design, executive talent assessment, CEO succession, and executive development.

As a thought leader in the field of organizational development, he has published 28 books and numerous articles, including *Designing Effective Organizations: The Sociotechnical Systems Perspective; Creating Strategic Change: Designing the Flexible, High-Performing Organization; Handbook of Collaborative*

Management Research (with Abraham B. Shani, Susan A. Morhman, Bengt Stymne, and Niclas Adler); and *Relationships That Enable Enterprise Change: Leveraging the Client-Consultant Connection* (with Ron A. Carucci). Bill has served as the editor of the *Journal of Applied Behavioral Science* and was a founding co-editor of the annual series *Research in Organizational Change and Development.*

Before joining the Center for Creative Leadership, Bill was a partner at Delta Consulting, and prior to that a tenured full professor at Case Western Reserve University and a visiting professor at Stanford and INSEAD. He resides in both New York City and Greensboro, North Carolina.

Center for
Creative
Leadership®

THE CENTER FOR CREATIVE LEADERSHIP (CCL) is a top-ranked global provider of executive education that unlocks individual and organizational potential through its exclusive focus on leadership education and research. The *Financial Times* has ranked CCL's public programs in the top 10 internationally for 10 consecutive years. Founded in 1970 as a nonprofit educational institution, CCL helps clients worldwide cultivate creative leadership—the capacity to achieve more than imagined by thinking and acting beyond boundaries—through an array of programs, products, and other services. CCL is headquartered in Greensboro, North Carolina, with campuses in Colorado Springs, Colorado; San Diego, California; Brussels, Belgium; and Singapore; and with offices in Pune, India, and Moscow, Russia. Supported by more than 400 faculty members and staff, it works annually with more than 20,000 leaders and 2,000 organizations. In addition, 12 network associates around the world offer selected CCL programs and assessments.

Berrett–Koehler
Publishers

Berrett-Koehler is an independent publisher dedicated to an ambitious mission: *connecting people and ideas to create a world that works for all*.

We believe that to truly create a better world, action is needed at all levels—individual, organizational, and societal. At the individual level, our publications help people align their lives with their values and with their aspirations for a better world. At the organizational level, our publications promote progressive leadership and management practices, socially responsible approaches to business, and humane and effective organizations. At the societal level, our publications advance social and economic justice, shared prosperity, sustainability, and new solutions to national and global issues.

A major theme of our publications is "Opening Up New Space." Berrett-Koehler titles challenge conventional thinking, introduce new ideas, and foster positive change. Their common quest is changing the underlying beliefs, mindsets, institutions, and structures that keep generating the same cycles of problems, no matter who our leaders are or what improvement programs we adopt.

We strive to practice what we preach—to operate our publishing company in line with the ideas in our books. At the core of our approach is stewardship, which we define as a deep sense of responsibility to administer the company for the benefit of all of our "stakeholder" groups: authors, customers, employees, investors, service providers, and the communities and environment around us.

We are grateful to the thousands of readers, authors, and other friends of the company who consider themselves to be part of the "BK Community." We hope that you, too, will join us in our mission.

A BK Business Book

This book is part of our BK Business series. BK Business titles pioneer new and progressive leadership and management practices in all types of public, private, and nonprofit organizations. They promote socially responsible approaches to business, innovative organizational change methods, and more humane and effective organizations.

Berrett–Koehler
Publishers

Connecting people and ideas
to create a world that works for all

Dear Reader,

Thank you for picking up this book and joining our worldwide community of Berrett-Koehler readers. We share ideas that bring positive change into people's lives, organizations, and society.

To welcome you, we'd like to offer you a free e-book. You can pick from among twelve of our bestselling books by entering the promotional code **BKP92E** here: http://www.bkconnection.com/welcome.

When you claim your free e-book, we'll also send you a copy of our e-newsletter, the *BK Communiqué*. Although you're free to unsubscribe, there are many benefits to sticking around. In every issue of our newsletter you'll find

- A free e-book
- Tips from famous authors
- Discounts on spotlight titles
- Hilarious insider publishing news
- A chance to win a prize for answering a riddle

Best of all, our readers tell us, "Your newsletter is the only one I actually read." So claim your gift today, and please stay in touch!

Sincerely,

Charlotte Ashlock
Steward of the BK Website

Questions? Comments? Contact me at bkcommunity@bkpub.com.